I0815041

ANDREY TARKOVSKY
LIFE AND WORK

The five feature films Andrey Tarkovsky (1932–1986) directed in the Soviet Union – among them *Andrei Rublev*, *Solaris*, and *Stalker* – brought him international fame. Evading censorship and mounting pressure by Soviet authorities, he did not return to the Soviet Union after completing *Nostalgia* in Tuscany in 1983. His final film, *The Sacrifice*, was shot in Sweden in 1985.

Compiled and edited by Tarkovsky's son Andrey Jr., film historian and critic Hans-Joachim Schlegel, and Lothar Schirmer, our book pays homage to a great visionary who thought in poetic and, at times, disturbing images of near biblical intensity. It features stills from each of his films, a selection of his own writings, private photographs from the family album, as well as Polaroids from Russia and Italy. Prominent voices who have commented on Tarkovsky's work and personality – including Jean-Paul Sartre, Ingmar Bergman, and Aleksandr Sokurov – round out the volume, now available in this low-price special edition.

288 pages, 350 illustrations in color and black-and-white
ISBN 978-3-8296-0811-4

Andrey Tarkovsky, 1979. Photo: Gueorgui Pinkhassov

ANDREY TARKOVSKY

LIFE AND WORK

Film by Film, Stills, Polaroids & Writings

EDITED BY
Andrey A. Tarkovsky Jr.
Hans-Joachim Schlegel
and Lothar Schirmer

ESSAY BY
Hans-Joachim Schlegel,
TEXTS BY
Andrey Tarkovsky
AND BY
Jean-Paul Sartre, Sven Nykvist,
Erland Josephson, Ingmar Bergman, Chingiz Aitmatov
and Aleksandr Sokurov

SCHIRMER/MOSEL

Translations from German and French by David H. Wilson.
Translations from Russian by Christine Barnard.

American edition of *Andrej Tarkovskij – Leben und Werk*
published by Schirmer/Mosel, Munich

For permission to include the film stills the publisher would like to thank
the following companies: Mosfilm, Moscow, for *Ivan's Childhood, Andrei Rublev,*
Solaris, Mirror and *Stalker*; Opera Film Produzione, Rome, for *Nostalgia*;
Svenska Filminstitutet, Stockholm, for *The Sacrifice.*

Separations: Bayermedia, Munich
Printed in Italy: EBS, Verona

ISBN 978-3-8296-0811-4

A Schirmer/Mosel Production
www.schirmer-mosel.com

Contents

‘Friends, today you are going to see something outstanding.
Something that has never been seen on our screens before.
But believe me: it shows a great talent!
The director’s name is Andrey Tarkovsky.’

Mikhail Romm, at the premiere of *Ivan’s Childhood* in 1962, quoted in Maya Turovskaya, *Tarkovsky: Cinema as Poetry*, 1989

Between Here and There

Andrey Tarkovsky's World of Pictures and Sounds

HANS-JOACHIM SCHLEGEL

On 25 May 1983 Andrey Tarkovsky was in Rome. He wrote in his diary: 'A very bad day. Depressing thoughts...Fear...I am lost...I can no longer live in Russia, but I can't live here either.' Homeless, between here and there, he was condemned to suffer that *nostalgia* – the chronic disease of the Russian in exile – which had been the subject of the first film he made abroad. He had been forced to leave Soviet Russia because of the humiliating bureaucratic restrictions imposed on his work by the longstanding chairman of Goskino, Filip Yermash. One reason for Yermash's hostility was Tarkovsky's individuality, both artistic and personal. Yermash dreamed of creating a Soviet Hollywood and so favoured directors of spectacular blockbusters such as Oscar winner Sergei Bondarchuk, whom he nominated to serve as a juror at Cannes, probably to ensure that Tarkovsky's *Nostalgia* was not awarded the Palme d'Or. For Tarkovsky, as he wrote in a letter to his father on 16 September 1983, that was 'the last straw'. He duly went into exile in Paris, where he died of cancer on 29 December 1986 – the day before Yermash was relegated to early retirement as Perestroika began to take hold.

The news that at long last the people of Russia would be allowed to see his films never reached Tarkovsky. But in any case, he was sceptical about the changes taking place in his home country. He felt some bitterness as he sensed the approaching canonization of his works and his person, though he knew it would be impossible to fight against it. With the posthumous award of the Order of Lenin and his semi-official rehabilitation, the pendulum swung from humiliation and exclusion to disproportionate adulation. This cult-like worship, along with his status as a political exile, distracted attention from the creative aspects of his work. The same happened outside Russia, too, where the poetic ambivalence, dreamlike landscapes of mist and rain and sublimely orchestrated soundscapes of his films encouraged a variety of pseudo-religious speculation.

During the quarter century or so since his death in Paris, Tarkovsky's films have been viewed and studied with ever greater interest. It is not only film fans who continue to discover new elements within them; scholars of art and cinema, theologians, philosophers and even psychologists have stepped beyond the confines of the filmic to draw parallels with their own disciplines. Perhaps most important of all, his work has been an inspiration to film-makers from other countries, cultures and beliefs. For Ingmar Bergman, who along with Robert Bresson, Luis Buñuel, Akira Kurosawa and Aleksandr Dovzhenko was among the directors Tarkovsky most admired when he was at film school, his place in film history was guaranteed by his peerless ability to 'grasp life as a vision, as a dream'. This was the quality that also inspired directors such as Theo Angelopoulos, Kenji Mizoguchi, Hou Hsiao-Hsien and Tsai Ming-Liang, Fred Kelemen, and the Iranian Panahbarkhoda Rezaee. In addition to such spiritually minded film-makers, another disciple was the Hungarian agnostic Béla Tarr, whose films *Damnation* (1988) and *Sátántangó* (1994) depict rainy, misty landscapes full of helplessly isolated people – transcendental hope giving way to the existential nothingness of man in all his nakedness.

Russia's acclaimed contemporary director Aleksandr Sokurov denies he was ever a pupil of Tarkovsky, although during his time in exile Tarkovsky did arrange for Sokurov to receive a bursary. In Sokurov's early work, however, Tarkovsky's influence is unmistakable, as in his debut feature *The Lonely Voice of Man* (1978), which Tarkovsky rated highly despite his criticism of the editing, or *Silent Pages*, a meditation on Dostoyevsky's

Crime and Punishment, or Sokurov's contemplative documentary films – especially *Oriental Elegy* (1996) – which give vivid cinematic expression to the transcendence of reality, the interweaving of this world and the next, and the quest for a spiritual union between home and elsewhere.

Tarkovsky intended his films to have multiple possible interpretations, and indeed in his last interview he explicitly welcomed the controversy aroused by *The Sacrifice*. Nothing would have pleased him less than a clear and universally accepted reading of his cinema, whose ambivalent, dreamlike logic the viewer is supposed to link through free association to his or her own dreams and traumas. These films hold their secrets – and so paradoxically have an openness of interpretation that attracts directors from other cultural, religious and philosophical backgrounds.

The texts and films Sokurov dedicated to Tarkovsky reveal a profound but not slavish admiration for the master.[1] For Sokurov, Tarkovsky was neither a god nor a revolutionary genius but simply a Russian who had suffered a tragic fate – and whom Sokurov also knew as a bit of a dandy and self-promoter.

By the time he was twenty-one, Tarkovsky had already fallen foul of the Soviet establishment through his eccentric style of dress and hipster (*stilyaga*) admiration for jazz and other elements of the Moscow subculture. In 1953, the year of Stalin's death, he broke off his studies in Arabic and joined a geological expedition to hunt for gold and diamonds along the wild Kureika river in the Far Eastern Turukhansk Taiga, a region to which Stalin himself had once been banished. Tarkovsky brought back sample stones along with sketches of Siberian landscapes that are now in the archives of the Moscow NIGRIzoloto Institute. His film-school work *Concentrate* captures impressions from this expedition.

All these experiences formed part of Tarkovsky's history and personality, which has often been reduced too narrowly to that of an introverted film-artist. His rebellious streak may have had its roots in his family: his grandfather, Aleksandr Karlovich Tarkovsky, was sentenced as a twenty-two-year-old Narodnaia Volia (People's Will) revolutionary to several years' imprisonment; his father – the esteemed lyric poet and translator Arseny Aleksandrovich Tarkovsky – was one of the circle of literary and ideological non-conformists surrounding the poets Marina Tsvetaeva and Anna Akhmatova. At VGIK in Moscow, Tarkovsky studied alongside the legendary 1960s directors of the 'Thaw' generation, whose individualistic, taboo-breaking films brought about a lasting change in Soviet cinema. In Marlen Khutsiev's semi-documentary feature *I Am Twenty* (1961),[2] we see Tarkovsky with a number of other young non-conformists discussing world views that betray no trace of conventional dogma. The topics include the relationship between poetry and technology, which was to become a theme of *Solaris* and *Stalker*.

Tarkovsky studied under Mikhail Romm, who expressly encouraged his students to develop their own creative talents, even if these led them in unexpected directions. With his diploma film *The Steamroller and the Violin* (1961), which already contains images that were to become central to his later works (a child, a mirror, an apple, a sudden downpour), Tarkovsky resolutely refused to be swayed by the objections raised by the studio. 'I cannot speak a dogmatic language,' was his response to criticism.

Right from the start, then, it seemed inevitable that he would come into permanent conflict with the state's administrators, whose interference in his work became more and more intolerable until he was finally driven into exile. But even then he insisted he was not a dissident, which alienated among others Vladimir Maximov, who organized the Milan press conference where on 10 July 1984 Tarkovsky publicly declared he would never return to the USSR.

Tarkovsky's reluctance to be pinned down by conventions or fixed meanings applied as much to his person as to his work. In discussions he would sometimes say one thing in the morning and another in the afternoon, then reconcile the two positions in the evening. He was astute enough to recognize kindred spirits among his opponents and he could also turn his back on long-standing friends and colleagues if he wished to explore new territories. He never shied away from radical ideas or from conflict and contradiction. In his book *Sculpting in Time: Reflections on the Cinema*,[3] he argues against the contemporary avant-garde, yet in his films he experimented with *musique concrète* (for instance, in the scene in *Nostalgia* where raindrops fall on bottles containing differing amounts of water). In the composition of his images, too, he repeatedly revealed himself to be an anti-avant-garde avant-gardist.

There can be no doubt that underlying Tarkovsky's opposition to avant-garde art and theory, materialist aesthetics, structuralism, semiotics and psychoanalysis was a stubborn, ever-present spirit of contradiction. He needed to adopt a position entirely his own, and to the annoyance of Western European intellectuals he would maintain it with a passion that sounded both pre-modern and anti-Enlightenment. Just as provocative was his attitude towards women, which oscillated between veneration and machismo; essentially, he associated them with 'submission, humiliation in the name of love'.[4] The ideas and values of modern Western Europe were as alien to him as the structures of its commercial film-production companies. He responded to both with a mixture of personal disgust and a more general criticism of Western culture.

In 1983 he told a correspondent from the German news magazine *Der Spiegel*: 'Here [in the West] money is the absolute ruler. This threatens creativity and is a menace to the whole future of the film industry. I never had such problems in the Soviet Union.'[5] Yet diary entries clearly reveal that he had continual money worries in the USSR, condemning him to accept commercial scripts and undertake lecture tours of the provinces. And of course the state-run Mosfilm studios allowed him a second chance that would have been inconceivable for a Western film company: after the original was discovered to be technically flawed, he was allowed to reshoot *Stalker*.

Filming on *The Sacrifice* was held up not by ideological disputes but by long-drawn-out financial problems, to which Tarkovsky reacted with a savage indictment of Western culture: 'Here in the West people are mainly preoccupied solely with themselves. If you tell them that the meaning of life lies in sacrificing oneself for others, they will probably laugh themselves silly and won't take you seriously. Nor will they believe you when you say that man was certainly not born solely to be happy. And that there are certainly more important things than personal success and commercial advantage. But obviously here in the West no one believes any more in the immortality of the soul.'

For Tarkovsky, market economy materialism was as great a 'betrayal of the spiritual mind' as the ideological materialism of official Soviet doctrine – which he continually managed to subvert in his films, despite the obstacles placed in his way. His criticisms of Western culture sometimes adopt an openly Slavonic tone, reminiscent of Dostoyevsky's anti-Western bias and recalling the rift between East and West that opened in 1054 with the Great Schism that split the Christian church. Time and again Tarkovsky contrasts Western rationality and pragmatism with *duhovnost*, the spirituality of the East. In a lecture entitled 'The Apocalypse', which he gave in London on 18 July 1984 at St James's Church, Piccadilly, he explicitly used the modern religious paintings in the Vatican Museum as a reference point for his criticism of contemporary art, which in his view 'has taken a wrong turn'.[6] This was the fault of the rational, analytical mindset of the West, which 'takes away the magic' of the creative act and so loses sight of its spiritual significance.

Tarkovsky believed that the 'mystique', the spirituality of his films, was inaccessible to a spectator who 'lost the capacity simply to surrender to an immediate, emotional aesthetic impression, that he instantly has to check himself, and ask: "Why? What for? What's the point?"'[7] His films could only be understood and fully experienced by a 'naïve' observer who allows free rein to his or her impressions, 'simply emotional, in a direct aesthetic sense'. 'The artist reveals his world to us, and forces us either to believe in it or to reject it as something irrelevant and unconvincing. In creating an image he subordinates his own thought, which becomes insignificant in the face of that emotionally perceived image of the world that has appeared to him like a revelation.'[8] This is why Tarkovsky rejected symbolic interpretations of his work. 'People have often asked me what the Zone is, and what it symbolizes, and have put forward wild conjectures on the subject. I'm reduced to a state of fury and despair by such questions. The Zone doesn't symbolize anything, any more than anything else does in my films: the zone is a zone...'[9] Instead of clearly decipherable symbols Tarkovsky reaches for the transcendental and magical, images of the kind he admired in the work of Russian symbolist Vyacheslav Ivanov, whom he quotes in *Sculpting in Time:* 'A symbol is only a true symbol when it is inexhaustible and unlimited in its meaning, when it utters in its arcane (hieratic and magical) language of hint and intimation something that cannot be set forth, that does not correspond to words. It has many faces and many thoughts, and in its remotest depths it remains inscrutable...'[10]

The Russian symbolists saw art as an antidote to the 'scientific systematization of ignorance', or as theurgy (divine intervention) which 'revives the power of myth' and leads to 'a catharsis for the human soul'. This was how Tarkovsky envisaged his own role, too – to such a degree that he applied the key precepts of Russian symbolism both literally and in spirit to *Sculpting in Time.* He too regarded the artist as a creator whose 'hieroglyphs of absolute truth' have a deeper and more substantial existential significance than the analytical 'discoveries' of science: 'Art could be said to be a symbol of the universe, being linked with that absolute spiritual truth which is hidden from us in our positivistic, pragmatic activities.'[11] There are parallels here with German romanticism, which fascinated Tarkovsky, inspiring him to write a film on the mystical aspects of the life and work of E. T. A. Hoffmann.[12] But the true source of his quest for artistic transcendence – for the absolute, the unseen and the unseeable – was the spiritual imagery characteristic of the Eastern Church, where the icon opened a window on the divine Logos, 'raising the spirit to an Ur-image'.[13] Here the icon was far more than a didactic illustration for the benefit of illiterate churchgoers – as Pope Gregory the Great saw it.

For Tarkovsky, icons were not just visual products of Russian culture – they embodied the soul of his country. They were not realistic portraits but rather were means of transcending borders. And in the same way, the images in his films do not set out to copy reality but instead seek to help us experience the invisible within the visible, the inner reality that lies within the outer.

Tarkovsky's films rarely contain actual icons. We see a few in the credits at the end of *Andrei Rublev* and as illustrations in a book in *The Sacrifice.* By contrast, there are many paintings from Western European art history, especially from the 15th and 16th centuries. In *Ivan's Childhood* there are pictures by Dürer – including his *Horsemen of the Apocalypse,* which Ivan, by now emotionally drained, relates to his own very real war traumas. In *Stalker* the image of John the Baptist from the Van Eyck brothers' Ghent altarpiece lies with coins, cannulas, a rusty submachine gun and other *objets trouvés* from a lost civilization in the gently flowing water of a newly awakened nature. Leonardo da Vinci is quoted in *Mirror* (*Portrait of Ginevra de' Benci*) and *The Sacrifice* (a fragment from *Adoration of the Magi*), Piero della Francesca's *Madonna Del Parto* forms part of the plot of *Nostalgia,* and in *Mirror* Tarkovsky creates images based on Pieter Bruegel's *Winter Landscape* and Philipp Otto Runge's *Portrait of a Boy.* None of these references is illustrative or symbolic, but they become integral elements within a spiritual, markedly Russian context. Tarkovsky searches the art of Western Europe's past for traces of a spirituality that has not yet been ruined by reason, for bridges with and alternatives to the art of the East, for signs of hope that his longing for a spiritual union between East and West might yet be fulfilled. A frequently repeated symbol for this is his discovery of a copy of the icon of the Virgin of Vladimir – a gift from an unknown Russian artist – on the altar of the 11th-century church of Portonovo in Italy.

In the final scene of *Nostalgia,* however, what we see in the nave of a ruined Italian church is not an icon but a Russian village landscape containing Tarkovsky's childhood home; his contemplative gaze is fixed not on some transcendental Great Beyond but on memories of his own past. Here, as in all his films, the main character is a poetic reflection of the director himself, an alter ego: 'The search for a style and a form is nothing else but a search for the expression of one's own self.'[14] In this too Tarkovsky breaks with the tenets of iconology, which according to canonical rules only allows copies of the original image; there must be no variation in even the minutest detail and individual interpretation is strictly forbidden. Even as he writes that the 'mystery of art' focuses on the 'absolute' (for Tarkovsky, a synonym for the divine), and the filmic image is a 'hieroglyph of eternal truth', Tarkovsky is secularizing the religious by placing it in a poetic dimension that is manifestly related to himself. Since man was created in the image of God, the spiritual artist may be proclaimed a 'harbinger of the absolute' and his films experienced like a 'church service'. He is a creator whom the observer must trust and believe in unconditionally, 'In just the same way, for a true faith in God, or even in order to feel a need for that faith, a person has to have a certain cast of soul, a particular spiritual potentiality.'[15]

Tarkovsky has often been called a Russian Orthodox director, but despite the religious allusions in his films, that is not what he was or what he wanted to be. In *Stalker* there are quotations from the Book of Revelation, the story of Christ's appearance on the road to Emmaus and a picture of John the Baptist, and the Writer – whether seriously or ironically – wears a crown of thorns. But all of this has an auratic or at least ambivalent function. Even in matters of religion, Tarkovsky refused to be pinned down. When asked about *The Sacrifice* in his last interview, he said: 'I don't think it's really important whether I adhere to any particular conviction or faith – heathen, Catholic, Protestant or Christian in general. What matters is the film.'[16] In *The Sacrifice* Alexander saves the world from an ongoing nuclear catastrophe not just through prayer to God but by a heathen, ritualistic sex act with a 'white witch' who bears the name of the Madonna: Mary. In the eyes of the church this was blasphemy. But Tarkovsky's attitude to the church contained both disappointment and reservations. In the closing chapter of *Sculpting in Time*, he states that '...not even the Church can quench a man's thirst for the Absolute, for unfortunately it only exists as a kind of appendage, copying or even caricaturing the social institutions by which our everyday life is organized.'[17]

Even before they had seen the film, the reactions of church officials to *Andrei Rublev* were wholly negative. The much revered 15th-century monk and icon painter is shown as being at odds not only with the world and his fellow humans, but also with God. He rebels against his conventional, ascetic teacher Theophanes the Greek and refuses to frighten his compatriots – already victims of violence, hunger and disease – with frescoes depicting future misery through the torments of hell. He wants 'to serve mankind, not God', and his passionate, angry love for his fellow men leads him to murder. Eventually, however, he breaks his silence, and his joy in the delights of earthly creation leads him to reverse his self-imposed ban on painting. Tarkovsky also aroused the wrath of the church by showing monks as informers for the ruling elite and as abusing the values of monastic life. There was particular revulsion at the depiction of an orgiastic, heathen rite of spring that included a scene in which the crucifixion seems to be subject to mockery.

As a student Tarkovsky was fascinated by the pantheistic scenes in Aleksandr Dovzhenko's collectivist film *Earth*. He was superstitious, and became deeply interested in parapsychology, esotericism and occultism. He believed his dead mother was sending him signals from beyond the grave to tell him she was looking after him; he went to séances to ask the ghost of Boris Pasternak to prophesy his fate as an artist; he became friendly with a Milanese professor of parapsychology. When the actor Anatoli Solonitsyn, who was a close friend, grew ill with cancer, Tarkovsky turned to the renowned faith healer Djuna Davitashvili – whom Leonid Brezhnev also consulted. When he himself was diagnosed with cancer he sought a cure at an anthroposophic clinic in Baden-Baden. Shortly before his death, his interest in anthroposophy led him to plan a film based on Rudolf Steiner's writings on the Gospels.

Tarkovsky's preoccupation with Zen Buddhism and Taoism also informed his work. He had read Otton

Ottonovich Rosenberg's *Die Probleme der buddhistischen Philosophie*, and *Sculpting in Time* ends with a reference to Taoist China: 'The East was closer to the truth than the West....Compare Eastern and Western music. The West is forever shouting, "This is me! Look at me! Listen to me suffering, loving! How unhappy I am! How happy! I! Mine! Me!" In the Eastern tradition they never utter a word about themselves. The person is totally absorbed into God, Nature, Time; finding himself in everything; discovering everything in himself. Think of Taoist music....China six hundred years before Christ...'[18] He believed Western civilization had long since 'swallowed' the spiritual East with its 'material demands on life', and the East remained as important a source of inspiration as Western European paintings of the 15th and 16th centuries or the music of Johann Sebastian Bach. Like the Russian eagle, he looked to both East and West with a mix of hope and scepticism. His attitude to Western Europe was as ambivalent as his attitude to Asia, with its memories of Russia's suffering under the yoke of the Mongols and the brutal attacks of the Tatars, as depicted so realistically in *Andrei Rublev*. References to the fight against the 'pan-Mongolian menace', from which Russia also protected Europe, are foregrounded in *Mirror*, where Tarkovsky quotes from a famous letter by Pushkin to Petr Chaadaev about Russia's role in defending European Christianity from Asia. And there is the current and ever-present menace evoked by documentary pictures of the Chinese-Soviet border conflict along the Ussuri river.

But there was also the Central Asia that offered fascinating locations and people, and the fifteen colleagues for whom Tarkovsky wrote film scripts (including the renowned Uzbek directors Ali Khamraev and Shukhrat Abbasov, the Kazakh film star Shaken Aimanov, and others with whom he and Kyrgyzstan writers Chingiz Aitmatov and Mukhtar Auezov collaborated). The elliptical, three-lined Japanese haiku became a model for his filmic language, as it had been for Sergei Eisenstein, whose 'intellectual montage' he vehemently criticized and often misunderstood. Above all, though, it was Asia's spiritual doctrines of Buddhism and Taoism that he drew inspiration from. In *The Sacrifice* it is these as much as Christian prayers and occult burial rituals that contain hope for a world already dedicated to its own destruction. Alongside the alto aria 'Erbarme Dich' from Bach's *St Matthew Passion* and Swedish folk music, we hear the sound of the ancient Japanese *hotchiku* flute. When in the final scene Alexander keeps the promise he made to God and burns down his house, he is wearing a kimono bearing the yin-yang symbol. The withered tree he planted at the beginning of the film as a material sign of hope – against all reason – provides an echo of oriental woodcuts and recalls a legend most likely to have originated in Asia.

The Taoist world view was especially meaningful to Tarkovsky because it focuses on the inner self rather than a transcendental Beyond. The idea that the contemplative spirit 'loses itself completely in God, in Nature, in time, and it finds itself again in all of that' formed the basis of his own thinking, and all his films are about the quest for the self – for the lost house of his childhood, for his own individually remembered time. He pursued this quest relentlessly, creating difficulties for himself as well as for his Soviet and foreign producers, public, friends and colleagues. Vadim Iusov, his cameraman for many years, refused to work on *Mirror*, which he regarded as 'immorally self-referential'; Andrei Konchalovsky, a friend since their student days and co-author of several film scripts, maintained that Tarkovsky's concern was not with '*istina*, eternal truth' at all, but solely with himself. The response of audiences, however, indicated that it was precisely this autobiographical, introverted, mysteriously associative 'mirror' that provided many Russians with a sense of *déjà vu*, with personal recollections that embodied the memories of a generation. And even outside Russia, this hermetic film touched the nerve of its audiences' subconscious.

While it was still being made, *Mirror* provided Tarkovsky's mother with an unusual experience of *déjà vu*. Since his aim was not only to evoke emotions but to reproduce real, concrete memories, he insisted on a completely accurate reconstruction of the lost house of his childhood, drawing on old photographs and even going so far as to sow buckwheat outside it, which grew and flourished, to the surprise of local farmers. His mother accepted the reconstruction as being her house. 'When we subsequently took my mother there, whose youth had been spent in that place and that house, her reaction to seeing it surpassed my boldest expectations. What she experienced was a return to her past; and then I knew we were moving in the right direction. The house awoke in her the feelings which the film was intended to express...'[19]

For Tarkovsky, the inner, poetic world was always inextricably linked to the real, material world, just as the icon gave material form to the transcendental through its colours, varnish and wood. A particularly important element in this association of visible and invisible, outer and inner, real and imaginary, originated in Asia. In the memoirs of the Soviet journalist and Japanese specialist Vsevolod Ovchinnikov, Tarkovsky came across the phenomenon of the *sabi*, the 'rust of time' inscribed into old, used objects. In *Sculpting in Time*, he quotes from Ovchinnikov: 'It is considered that time, *per se*, helps to make known the essence of things. The Japanese therefore see a particular charm in the evidence of old age. They are attracted to the darkened tone of an old tree, the ruggedness of a stone, or even the scruffy look of a picture whose edges have been handled by a great many people. To all these signs of age they give the name, *saba*, which literally means "rust". *Saba*, then, is a natural rustiness, the charm of olden days, the stamp of time. [– or patina – *A.T.*]'[20] Tarkovsky's intense interest in this phenomenon was shared by Prague surrealist animator and artist Jan Švankmajer, who was fascinated by the 'latent content' of old everyday objects with their 'memories far transcending human memory'.[21] Despite his opposition to the surrealist avant-garde, the magic of time inscribed into concrete reality fired Tarkovsky's imagination. 'The magic, the seal, the patina of time' became of such importance that he titled his thoughts on the art, aesthetics and poetics of film *Sculpting in Time*.

The book's original Russian title, *Zapecatlënnoie vremia*, is difficult to translate. The words allude to two very different ideas: the 'fixed' time captured on film and the time locked away beneath the seal of the secret apocalyptic mystery. As we were walking together on the western side of the Glienicke Bridge in Berlin, Tarkovsky gave me an indirect insight into the significance of this apparent contradiction. I drew his attention to the weathered Cyrillic letters Soviet soldiers had scratched into the stonework in 1945, forming a sentence that might have come from Aleksandr Blok's poem *The Scythians*: 'The Scythians also came here.' Tarkovsky's reaction was electric. He touched the letters with his fingers like some kind of Doubting Thomas demanding to dip his finger into the resurrected Christ's stigmata. It was as if by making tactile contact with reality through the traces of the past left in the stone of the bridge, he was bringing that time back to life. These remnants of the past, material and tangible, sparked his imagination, opening a door from the here and now into the then of wartime, a traumatic part of his early years and, since *Ivan's Childhood*, a leitmotif in his films.

Remembered time is not fictive time – it is the imagined return of real, emotionally experienced time, not only through things that actually happened but through our reactions to stories and records of historical reality. Tarkovsky's images focus in particular on authentic, documentary 'fixed' time as captured on film. In *Mirror*, in the midst of poetically imagined personal experiences, we are repeatedly confronted by extracts from news bulletins – scenes from the Spanish Civil War or Second World War, atom-bomb tests on Bikini Atoll, Chinese-Russian border clashes along the Ussuri river. These are not aids to temporal orientation but rather integral components of Tarkovsky's individually imagined time. They are authentic documents which must have struck a deep chord and which he handles in a subjective, emotional way. Unlike in *Ivan's Childhood*, the Second World War in *Mirror* figures not only through film of the triumphant conquest of Berlin but through footage of the traumatically painful steps along the way – in other words, the journey that formed the subject matter of *Ivan's Childhood*.

Tarkovsky watched numerous films from the archives until at last he came upon an eleven-minute sequence showing exhausted Red Army soldiers wading through the muddy shallows of Lake Sivash. This provided a real-life emotional parallel with the key scene in *Ivan's Childhood* where the twelve-year-old protagonist wades through a swampy no-man's-land to the German front line. 'I had to look through thousands of metres of film before hitting on the sequence of the Soviet Army crossing Lake Sivash; and it stunned me....When, on the screen before me, there appeared, as if coming out of nothing, these people shattered by the fearful, inhuman effort of that tragic moment of history, I knew that this episode had to become the centre, the very essence, heart, nerve of this picture that had started off merely as my intimate lyrical memories.'[22]

The possibility of fixing time directly – i.e., not staging or editing anything – fascinated Tarkovsky so much that he eventually declared long-term documentary observation to be his ideal: 'I see chronicle as the ultimate cinema; for me it is not a way of filming but a way of reconstructing, of recreating life....This is how I conceive an ideal piece of filming: the author takes millions of metres of film, on which systematically, second by second, day by day and year by year, a man's life, for instance, from birth to death, is followed and recorded...'[23] But this idea was as impossible to realize as the plans he considered during his preparations for *Mirror*: to use a hidden camera to record his mother's conversations with a psychiatrist, or to 'translate' one of his father's poems into a short film. So he turned to 'found footage', which he selected according to purely subjective criteria to make it the 'nerve-centre, the heart' of the surrounding film.

Tarkovsky also used subjective criteria to select authentic sounds. One of his earliest experiments was in the Soviet radio sound studios in Moscow, when during the interminable delays before shooting *Andrei Rublev* he directed an adaptation of William Faulkner's short story 'Turnabout'. Because of its 'pacifist leanings', the play was given only one token night-time broadcast in the Transural region. It tells the story of a young English naval officer named Hope (played by actor and director Nikita Mikhalkov) who during the First World War is obsessed to the point of self-destruction with a plan to blow up the German fleet at Kiel. Tarkovsky was intrigued by the subject matter, which was similar to that of *Ivan's Childhood*. But he also saw the adaptation as an opportunity to experiment with his composer Vyacheslav Ovchinnikov on different ways of using sound for *Andrei Rublev*.

Most of the music for the radio play was orchestral, but Moscow radio historian Aleksandr Scherel also recalls Tarkovsky's keen interest in working with original sounds. As he was to do in *The Sacrifice*, Tarkovsky wanted to incorporate the cries of seagulls. These were no doubt available in the sound archives but Tarkovsky refused to rely on 'canned sound', insisting instead on taking an unwieldy Reportjor tape recorder to Jūrmala, on the east coast near Riga, where – as he put it – he could record his 'own' seagull cries. Not any old cries, but those that touched his emotions, that fitted with his particular sense of how the radio play should sound. And he didn't find them straight away – it took much wandering up and down the beach before he heard the right screeches.

The process exemplified by the long search through the archives to find the documentary footage of Red Army soldiers wading through the morass of Lake Sivash was to be repeated many times in Tarkovsky's quest for sounds. Whether sounds or images, he had to find the material that aroused a personal emotional response, and only then could it become an integral part of his imaginative blending of poetry and reality, of inner and outer truths. Sounds from nature that elicited an echo within himself became so important that for *Solaris* he parted company with Vyacheslav Ovchinnikov, the composer with whom he had collaborated since his diploma film *The Steamroller and the Violin*. From now on he would develop his ideas of cinematic sound mainly with Eduard Artemiev, who worked with electronic synthesizers. At their first meeting Tarkovsky said 'that "music as such" was of no use at all to him in his films, and the job consisted more in arranging natural sounds, perhaps reworking them through the tones and rhythms of the synthesizer, and enriching these natural sounds by means of some kind of musical material that would endow them with an individual and specific emotional expressiveness.'[24] Referring to his work with Artemiev on *Mirror*, Tarkovsky wrote in *Sculpting in Time*: 'Electronic music seems to me to have enormously rich possibilities for cinema. Artemiev and I used it in some scenes in *Mirror*.

'We wanted the sound to be close to that of an earthly echo, filled with poetic suggestion – to rustling, to sighing. The notes had to convey the fact that reality is conditional, and at the same time accurately to reproduce precise states of mind, the sounds of a person's interior world. The moment we hear what it is, and realize that it's being constructed, electronic music dies; and Artemiev had to use very complex devices to achieve the sounds we wanted. Electronic music must be purged of its "chemical" origins, so that as we listen we may catch in it the primary notes of the world.

'Instrumental music is artistically so autonomous that it is far harder for it to dissolve into the film to the point where it becomes an organic part of it. Therefore its use will always involve some measure of compromise, because it is always illustrative. Furthermore, electronic music has exactly that capacity for being absorbed into the sound. It can be hidden behind other noises and remain indistinct; like the voice of nature, of vague intimations...It can be like somebody breathing.'[25]

Tarkovsky's liking for authentic, unstaged sounds eventually led him to dispense completely with fictive musical accompaniments. 'It may be that in order to make the cinematic image sound authentically, in its full diapason, music has to be abandoned. For strictly speaking the world as transformed by cinema and the world as transformed by music are parallel, and conflict with each other. Properly organized in a film, the resonant world is musical in its essence....Above all, I feel that the sounds of this world are so beautiful in themselves that if only we could learn to listen to them properly, cinema would have no need of music at all.'[26]

The sound of rain, gusts of wind heralding dreams or traumas, the cuckoo's call like a distant echo of childhood – all these, together with Artemiev's electronic synthesizer, are part of the memorable acoustic experience of Tarkovsky's cinema. But in the end the switch from orchestral music to 'sound symphonies' remained a distant ideal as impossible to achieve as the concept of an unedited film of a lifetime's experiences. Even in *Solaris* Artemiev used a variation on Bach's *Prelude in F Minor*. In *Mirror*, as well as electronic sounds, there are quotations from Purcell and Pergolesi. In *Nostalgia* we hear not only the 'raindrop concerto' mentioned above but also music by Debussy, Verdi, Wagner and Beethoven. In *The Sacrifice* the themes are underscored by the alto aria 'Erbarme Dich' from Bach's *St Matthew Passion*, ancient Japanese flute and instrumental music, and Swedish folk music. Tarkovsky's ambivalence towards orchestral music is evident in the last scenes of *Stalker*, where the clatter of a passing train overlays and obliterates the 'Ode to Joy' from Beethoven's *Symphony No. 9*. The destructive threat of relentless technological pragmatism to human hopes is experienced here through sound, in contrast to *Nostalgia* and *The Sacrifice*, where it is explicitly the films' subject matter.

The world of sound had always been important to Tarkovsky. Even as an eleven-year-old he attended violin and piano lessons at a Moscow music school. His original ambition was to be a conductor, which he described as 'an ever-present dream to bring order and organization to chaos'. In 1983 he directed a production of Mussorgsky's *Boris Godunov* at the Royal Opera House in London's Covent Garden, under the baton of Claudio Abbado. During the last years of his life he could not live 'a single day without Bach'.

For Tarkovsky, sounds and music were never just an 'acoustic carpet' or decorative addition to his images; they were always an integral part of the film's auratic structure. He saw moving pictures and sound as having a close relationship: 'I classify cinema and music among the *immediate* art forms since they need no mediating language. This fundamental determining factor marks the kinship between music and cinema...'[27] The common denominator that binds moving pictures and sound is rhythm, which organizes 'chaos' and, above all, time: 'Rhythm, then, is not the metrical sequences of pieces; what makes it is the time-thrust within the frames. And I am convinced that it is rhythm, and not editing, as people tend to think, that is the main formative element of cinema.'[28] While this is not a new insight, Tarkovsky's originality lay in his emphasis on subjectivity. He defined rhythm as the manifestation of a particular 'sense' of time, in which a director's 'individuality' found its expression,[29] and it was in this way that he defined his art as 'sculpting in time'.[30] For Tarkovsky, time was 'the flame in which there lives the salamander of the human soul.'[31] It was not a generally valid norm but an individual perception – an inner time. In his films he wanted to 'create [his] own, distinctive flow of time, and convey in the shot a sense of its movement – from lazy to soporific to stormy and swift – and to one person it will seem one way, to another, another.'[32]

This 'feeling of time' is, of course, especially evident in the autobiographical film *Mirror*. But so too is Tarkovsky's imaginative concept of historical time. Right from the start *Andrei Rublev* was not intended to be a 'historical or biographical work. I was interested in something else: I wanted to investigate the nature of the poetic genius of the great Russian painter. I wanted to use the example of Rublev to explore the question of the psychology of artistic creativity, and analyse the mentality and civic awareness of an artist who created spiritual treasures of timeless significance.'[33] So Tarkovsky was interested in Rublev not as a canonized saint of the Russian Orthodox Church but as an artist whose creative spirituality took him beyond norms and dogmas, and who saw his own sufferings as a necessary sacrifice in the service of his fellow-sufferers. In the end, Rublev was Tarkovsky's poetic alter ego. The original title of the film was *Andrei's Passion*, which provides a clear indication of the director's identification with the hero.

Tarkovsky's individualistic and imaginative handling of historical time inevitably brought him into conflict with official versions of history. *Andrei Rublev* depicts 15th-century Russia as torn apart by Tatar invasions and brutal rulers, with conflicts between power-hungry brothers, treachery, famine and disease, its people demoralized and without hope. This alone was enough to provoke the wrath of official Soviet historians and the Slav-loving champions of 'Great Russia'. Even Aleksandr Solzhenitsyn – whom Tarkovsky greatly admired and whose Gulag novel *One Day in the Life of Ivan Denisovich* he wanted to film – wrote a paper while in exile in Vermont attacking this 'mockery and debasement of our history', of Andrei Rublev himself and of Russian Orthodoxy.[34]

The main characters in Tarkovsky's last two films have first names and situations that clearly reference their director. Andrei Gorchakov suffers from the same nostalgia in Italy as Tarkovsky did himself; in *The Sacrifice* Alexander, the namesake of Alexei, the authorial narrator of the autobiographical *Mirror*, is a theatre critic who flees to a remote island to escape the vanities of city life and culture. Both are poetic projections of the director. That the links to his own life are so clear and current changes the texture of the films, with poetic ambivalence and spiritual mystery increasingly giving way to something more overt. We see this for the first time in *Nostalgia*, where the 'holy madman' Domenico calls for a return to the old values and, in despair at a 'civilization that has gone crazy', burns himself alive in front of the Roman equestrian statue of Marcus Aurelius. *The Sacrifice* at times comes close to being a direct personal confession.

The idea for this film first came to Tarkovsky while he was still in Moscow and learned that his close friend and colleague Anatoli Solonitsyn had died of cancer. After Andrei Rublev, Hamlet, and his roles in *Solaris* (Sartorius), *Stalker* (Writer) and *Mirror* (Forensic Doctor), Solonitsyn was due to take the lead roles in *Nostalgia* and *The Sacrifice*. Originally *The Sacrifice* was to be a film about the last days of a writer dying of cancer, but now its subject matter became the fatal disease of a 'civilization that has gone crazy', and Tarkovsky was to make the film while suffering the extreme physical and psychological distress of his own cancer.

Intimations of his imminent death and a foreshadowing of the nuclear catastrophe at Chernobyl are interwoven with his dark, apocalyptic view of a civilization in decline that could be saved only by some kind of miracle. Alexander is prepared to make an almost Christ-like sacrifice to this end: he is willing to offer himself and the components that make up his identity to atone for the deadly sins of the world. Like Andrei Rublev, he takes a vow of silence and renounces everything that is most precious to him. Like Domenico, he becomes a 'holy madman' who burns down both his real house and that which lies within him – an act of profound symbolic significance to Tarkovsky. What goes up in flames is the wooden country house that recurs again and again in Tarkovsky's films as the nostalgic image of an inner *locus amoenus*, a lost harmony and security, a longed-for spiritual home and a true identity. And it burns at a moment when Tarkovsky himself was tormented by his apocalyptic vision of a world heading towards its end as well as by his own approaching death.

When *The Sacrifice* had its premiere at Cannes, where Tarkovsky's son Andrey Andreyevich accepted the jury prize on behalf of his father, who was now seriously ill, the clouds from Chernobyl were already over Europe. This gave the film an almost prophetic aura. The poetic ambivalence of Tarkovsky's cinematic language was now overlaid with an all too obvious despair. Ingmar Bergman described *Nostalgia* and *The Sacrifice* as 'films à la Tarkovsky', because for him Tarkovsky's 'greatness' and place in film history lay in the fact that 'he has brought to the cinema a new and special language, which allowed him to grasp life as a vision, as a dream.' It is precisely this vision that has made Andrey Tarkovsky so influential today, not only for cinema-goers but also for those directors who continue to draw from his work new ideas for films that reach beyond the triviality of the global mainstream.

1 See Sokurov's essay 'The Banal Egalitarianism of Death' in this volume, pp. 25–31, and also Sokurov's film *Moscow Elegy* (1986–87).
2 Because of a personal intervention by Nikita Khrushchev, the original uncut version, *The Ilyich Gate*, was banned for several years.
3 Andrey Tarkovsky, *Sculpting in Time: Reflections on the Cinema*, London, 1986, translated by Kitty Hunter-Blair.
4 Andrey Tarkovsky, *Time Within Time: The Diaries 1970–1986*, translated by Kitty Hunter-Blair, Calcutta, 1991, p. 89.
5 *Der Spiegel*, 7 February 1983.
6 *Sculpting in Time*, p. 38.
7 Ibid., p. 213.
8 Ibid., p. 41.
9 Ibid., p. 200.
10 Ibid., p. 47.
11 Ibid., p. 37.
12 *Hoffmanniana*. See *Andrei Tarkovsky: Collected Screenplays*, translated by William Powell and Natasha Synessios, London, 1999.
13 See Pavel Florensky, *Iconostasis*, New York, 1997.
14 Andrei Tarkovskij, *Martyrolog II. Tagebücher 1981–1986*, translated into German by Kurt Baudisch and Ute Spengler, Berlin, 1989, p. 272.
15 *Sculpting in Time*, p. 42.
16 *Iskusstvo Kino*, 1989/2, p. 144.
17 *Sculpting in Time*, p. 223.
18 Ibid., p. 226.
19 Ibid., p. 132.
20 Ibid., p. 59.
21 Quoted by Hans-Joachim Schlegel in 'Jan Svankmayer: Die subversive Macht der Imagination', in Ursula Blickle (ed.), *The Cabinet of Jan Svankmajer*, Nuremberg, 2011, p. 14.
22 *Sculpting in Time*, p. 130.
23 Ibid., pp. 64–65.
24 Translated from Eduard Artemiev, 'On dal nine polnuiu svobodu', in A. M. Sandler (ed.), *Miri filmy Andreja Tarkosgovo*, Moscow, 1991, p. 364 f.
25 *Sculpting in Time*, pp. 162–63.
26 Ibid., pp. 159–62.
27 Ibid., p. 176.
28 Ibid., p. 119.
29 Ibid., p. 120.
30 Ibid., p. 121.
31 Ibid., p. 57.
32 Ibid., pp. 120–21.
33 Ibid., p. 34.
34 Aleksandr Solzhenitsyn, 'Film o Rubleve', in *Vestnik Russkogo studencheskogo khristiansklgo dvizheniia*, 1984, no. 141.

Other Writers on Tarkovsky

JEAN-PAUL SARTRE
Discussion on the criticism of *Ivan's Childhood*

My dear Alicata,
I have told you many times how much I respect those of your colleagues who write about literature, the visual arts and cinema. I find their approach combines thoroughness with open-mindedness, enabling them in most cases to get to the heart of a problem while at the same time appreciating what is individual and concrete within a particular work. I can offer the same praise for *Il Paese* and *Paese Sera*: no leanings to the left, and no one with an agenda.

This is why I would like to express a regret: why is it, for the first time I can remember, that the accusation of bias can be levelled at the articles *L'Unità* and other journals of the left have published on *Ivan's Childhood*, one of the finest films I have had the privilege of seeing over the last few years? The film was awarded the Golden Lion by the Venice Film Festival jury, yet this accolade has been read as some strange certificate of 'Occidentalism', placing Tarkovsky under suspicion of being a *petit bourgeois* viewed with horror by the Italian left. Such sceptical readings, without any real justification, relinquish a profoundly Russian and Revolutionary film – a film that exemplifies and expresses the feelings of the younger generation of Soviets – to our middle classes. I myself saw *Ivan's Childhood* at a private screening in Moscow, where I understood what the film means to young people in their twenties, the heirs of the Revolution, whose values they uphold and intend to continue: in their approval of the film, I can assure you, there was nothing that could be described as *petit bourgeois*. Of course, a critic is free to express reservations about a work he or she has been asked to judge. But is it fair to show such disdain for a film which in Russia has been, and still is, the subject of passionate debate? Is it fair to criticize it *without taking into account* these discussions, as if *Ivan's Childhood* were nothing but an example of current film production in the USSR? I know you well enough, dear Alicata, to realize that you do not share the simplistic views of your critics. And as the respect I have for them is sincere, I ask you to let them see this letter, which may at the very least provide the opportunity to reopen discussion before it is too late.

They have spoken of traditionalism and, at the same time, of expressionism and an outmoded symbolism. Allow me to say that such formalist categories are themselves outmoded. It is true that symbolism is hidden below the surface in the work of Fellini and Antonioni, but this concealment only makes it more dazzling. And the Italian neo-realists did not reject symbolism either. I could talk here about the symbolic function of any work of art, even the most realistic, but unfortunately I do not have time. In any case, it is the *nature* of Tarkovsky's symbolism they wish to criticize: his symbols are supposedly expressionist or surrealist! This is what I cannot accept. First, because here again, as in the USSR, accusations of a near-obsolete academicism are levelled at the young director. For your best critics here, as for some critics there, it would seem Tarkovsky has rushed to assimilate ideas already out of date in the West, and has applied them without discernment. He is castigated for showing Ivan's dreams: 'Dreams! We in the West have long since given up using dreams! Tarkovsky is way behind: that was fine between the wars!' That is what has been written by those in authority.

But Tarkovsky is twenty-eight years old (he told me so himself – not thirty, as some newspapers have reported) and you can be sure that he knows very little about Western cinema. His culture is essentially and necessarily Soviet. There is nothing to gain and everything to lose by attributing 'bourgeois' ideas to a 'treatment' that arises directly from the film and its subject matter. Ivan is mad, he is a monster, he is a little hero. The truth is, he is the most innocent and moving victim of war: this boy, whom one cannot help liking, has been formed by violence. He has assimilated it. The Nazis killed him when they killed his mother and massacred the inhabitants of his village. And yet he is alive...but *somewhere else*, within that fatal moment when he saw the fall of his nearest and dearest. I myself have seen the hallucinations experienced by young Algerians scarred by the massacres they have witnessed. For them, there was no difference between the nightmare of the past and the nightmares they endured every night. They had been killed, they wanted to kill, and they wanted to be killed. Their heroic dedication was mainly to hatred and an escape from unbearable pain. If they fought, it was to escape the horror through fighting; if the night disarmed them, if in their sleep they returned to the tenderness of their youth, the horror was reborn and they relived the memories they strove to forget. Ivan is one of them. And I think we should praise Tarkovsky for having shown so vividly how, for this child on the verge of suicide, there is no difference between day and night. Ivan does not live in our world. For him, actions and hallucinations are inextricably linked. Look at the relationships he has with adults. He is surrounded by soldiers; officers – good people, brave but 'normal', who have not suffered a tragic childhood – welcome him, look after him, love him, would do anything to 'normalize' him, to send him back to school. It appears that the child might – as in Sholokhov's novel – find a father among them to replace the one he has lost. But it's too late – he no longer needs parents. And even more profound than this deprivation is the ineffable horror of the massacre he has witnessed, which drives him to solitude. The officers end up treating the child with a mix of tenderness, bewilderment and painful mistrust: they see in him the perfect monster, so handsome and so despicable, whom the enemy has *radicalized*, who can only express himself through murderous impulses (for instance, with the knife), who cannot break the bonds of war and death, who now needs this terrible world in order to live, who is free from fear in the midst of battle, and who if he were left behind would be consumed by terror. The little victim knows what he needs: war, which has created him, blood, and vengeance. And yet the two officers love him – and for his part all one can say is that he does not hate them. Love for him is a road forever blocked. So his nightmares and hallucinations are in no way gratuitous: these are not purple passages, nor are they explorations of the child's 'subjectivity' – they remain completely objective, and we continue to see Ivan from the outside, exactly as we do in the 'realistic' scenes. The truth is that for this child the whole world is an hallucination, and this same child, both monster and martyr, in this world is *an hallucination for everyone else*. That is why the first sequence cleverly introduces us to the true and false world of the boy and war by showing us everything, starting with his real journey through the forest and finishing with the false death of his mother (she is really dead, but the event – which we shall never see because it is too deeply buried – was different; it never returns to the surface except through transformations that omit some of its horrific nakedness). Madness? Reality? It is both: in war all soldiers are mad, and this child-monster bears objective witness to their madness, because he is the maddest of them all. And so this is not a matter of expressionism or symbolism but a means of story-telling imposed by the subject, which the young poet Voznesensky has called 'socialist surrealism'.

It is necessary to delve more deeply into the director's intentions to understand the true meaning of his subject matter: war kills everyone, even those who survive it. And in an even more profound sense, history shapes its own heroes, creating and destroying them by rendering them incapable of living without suffering in the society they have helped to form.

*A Man for Burning** has been acclaimed by critics while *Ivan's Childhood* has been received with suspicion. The authors of *A Man for Burning* have been praised because they introduced complexities into their positive hero. It is true they gave him some faults – mythomania, for instance. They also highlighted the character's devotion to the cause he is defending and his authentic egocentricity. But I can't find anything truly original in this. In the end, despite everything, the best products of social realism have always given us complex, subtly delineated heroes, exalting their good qualities while carefully drawing attention to certain weaknesses. In truth, the problem is not to weigh up the vices and virtues of the hero, but to discuss heroism itself – not in order to reject it, but in order to understand it. *Ivan's Childhood* sheds light simultaneously on its necessity and its ambiguity. The child has no trivial virtues or vices: right down to his roots he is what history has made him. Thrown into war despite himself, he is now constructed entirely for war. But if he scares the soldiers around him, it is because he will never be able to live in peace. The violence within him, born of terror and horror, sustains him, helps him to live, and drives him to embark on dangerous reconnaissance missions. But what will become of him after the war? If he survives, the burning lava inside him will never cool. Is this not – in the narrowest sense of the term – a *critique* of the positive hero? Ivan is shown just as he is, suffering and magnificent; we are allowed to see the tragic and deadly sources of his strength; we become aware that this product of war, perfectly adapted to the warrior society, is condemned because of this to become asocial in a world of peace. This is how history forms people: it chooses them, sits in the saddle, and then rides them to destruction. In the midst of men of peace, who are willing to die for peace and who make war for peace, this mad martial child makes war for the sake of war. That is why, even among the soldiers who love him, he lives in unendurable solitude.

And yet he is a child. This desolate soul still has the tenderness of childhood, even if he can no longer feel it, let alone express it. Or if he abandons himself to it in his dreams, or begins to dream among the gentle distractions of everyday tasks, we can be sure these dreams will inevitably turn into nightmares. Even simple images of everyday happiness make us afraid: we know how it will all end. Nevertheless, this suppressed and shattered tenderness is there throughout: Tarkovsky has taken care to surround Ivan with it. It is the world – the world in spite of the war and even sometimes because of it (I am thinking of those wonderful skies criss-crossed by fireballs). Indeed, the lyricism of the film, its lacerated sky, its quiet waters, its vast forests – these all make up Ivan's life, and the love and the roots he has been deprived of. They are what he was, and what he still is, although he cannot remember it. They are what others see in him, though he himself cannot see them. I know of nothing more moving than that extended sequence of crossing the river: long, slow, heart-rending. Despite their fear and uncertainty (was it right to make a child run such risks?), the officers accompanying him are overwhelmed by a desolate and terrible tenderness. But the child, obsessed with death, notices nothing, leaps on to the dry land and disappears, heading straight for the enemy. The boat returns to the other side; silence reigns in the middle of the river; even the cannon is silent. One soldier says to the other: 'This silence, it is war...'

Then at that very moment the silence explodes: shouts and cheers, it is peace. The Soviet soldiers, delirious with joy, have taken the Reichstag in Berlin, and go racing up the stairs. One of the officers – is the other dead? – has found some notebooks in a cupboard; the Third Reich was bureaucratic and for every person hanged there is a photograph and a name on a list. On one of these lists the young officer sees a photograph of

* *Un uomo da bruciare* (*A Man for Burning*) is a 1962 drama about the Sicilian Mafia, directed by Paolo and Vittorio Taviani and Valentino Orsini.

Ivan. Hanged at the age of twelve. In the midst of the joy of a nation that has paid dearly for the right to pursue the construction of socialism, there is a black hole – one among so many – a pinprick that cannot be healed: the death of a child in hatred and despair. Nothing, not even future Communism, will ever make up for that. Nothing. Here we are shown, without any intermediary, both collective joy and a small personal disaster. There is not even a mother to temper grief with pride. This is unadulterated loss. Human society advances towards its goals, the living will achieve their ends, yet this little death, a tiny wisp swept away by history, remains like an unanswered question, posing no threat but allowing us to see everything in a new light: history is tragic. Hegel said it. And also Marx, who added that history always progresses by its bad side. But in recent times we have hardly ever said such a thing, we have insisted on progress, forgetting the losses nothing can compensate us for. *Ivan's Childhood* reminds us of all that, in the most subtle, gentle and explosive manner. A child dies – and this is almost a happy ending, because he could not have survived. I think the director, this very young man, set out to speak for himself and for his generation. These young, proud, tough pioneers did not die – on the contrary – but their childhoods were shattered by the war and its consequences. You could almost say this is the Soviet equivalent of *Les quatre cents coups** – but I would want to emphasize the differences between the two films. A child torn to pieces by his parents – that is the bourgeois tragicomedy. Thousands of children destroyed alive by war – that is one of the Soviet tragedies.

It is in this sense that the film seems to me to be specifically Russian. The techniques it uses are certainly Russian, although they are original too. Here in the West we can appreciate the fast-moving, elliptical rhythms of Godard, the protoplasmic slowness of Antonioni. But the originality in *Ivan's Childhood* lies in seeing both paces used by a director who has been inspired by neither of these auteurs, but who wanted his audience to live through wartime with its unbearable slowness as well as to leap from one timeframe to another with the elliptical speed of history (I am thinking particularly of the contrast between the two sequences of the river and the Reichstag); he achieves this not through plot development but by leaving his characters at a particular moment in their lives and coming back to them at another, or even at their death. But this contrast of rhythms is not what gives the film its special character from a social point of view. During that same period, we all experienced some of those moments of despair that destroy a person. (I remember a Jewish boy of Ivan's age who, when he learned in 1945 that his mother and father had died in the gas chamber and been incinerated, poured petrol on his mattress, lay down on it, set fire to it and burned himself alive.) But we have had neither the opportunity nor the satisfaction of embarking upon a grandiose construction. We often encountered Evil. But never radical Evil in the midst of Good, at the moment when one enters into battle with Good itself. That is what is so striking here. Of course, no Soviet can say he or she is responsible for the death of Ivan; the only guilty parties are the Nazis. But that is not the problem: no matter where this Evil comes from, when it pierces Good with its countless needles, it reveals the tragic truth about man and historical progress. And where could that be better expressed than in the USSR, the only great country where the word progress has some meaning? There is no need to extrapolate from that some kind of pessimism or even a facile optimism. All we have is the will to fight, without losing sight of the price that must be paid. I know that you, dear Alicata, are even more aware than myself of the tears, sweat, and often blood that are the price of even the smallest change one wishes to make to society; I am sure you appreciate as much as I do this film on the irremediable losses of history. And the respect I have for the critics of *L'Unità* persuades me

* *Les quatre cents coups* (*The 400 Blows*) is a 1959 film directed by François Truffaut.

to ask you to show them this letter. I would be happy if some of these comments were to spur them into replying and reopening the discussion on *Ivan*. It is not the Golden Lion that should be Tarkovsky's true reward, but the interest – even if polemical – aroused by his film among those who themselves are fighting for the liberation of man and against war.

With very best wishes.

October 1962

First published in Italian in the newspaper *L'Unità*, 9 October 1963. Published in French in Jean-Paul Sartre, *Situations*, vol. VII, Paris: Gallimard, 1965.

SVEN NYKVIST

It is not the number of lights that make a picture impressive. Just the opposite, you create atmosphere with as little light as possible. Tarkovsky is enormously sensitive to light – but he's even more interested in the picture itself, of the movement with it...His style of directing is something I had never met before. He can't, or won't, express his intentions for pictures and scenes without having first searched his way through the camera – my camera!

He makes his films by way of the camera. This upset me at first. I thought he was taking over *my* job. But we had a frank talk about it and he explained that he always builds up his scenes like this. And of course he trusted me with everything pertaining to the photography. It was the choreography itself he did through the camera. When Andrey and I eventually saw eye to eye everything was easy, well-organized and self-evident. I became as one with him and his intentions, and there were no more obstacles, no more jagged nerves, only fascination and pleasure.

One of the most vital items in a cameraman's baggage is the ability to adapt himself, to seek a style, which although personal in every film, is set within the frame of the film he's working on.

Tarkovsky's ideas of a take are different from those of most other directors. He doesn't break it up into long shots, medium close-ups and close-ups. His compositions are unconventional. His cameras move, his actors move and there's an impressive amount of action in his scenes.

I have always striven for simplification. The simpler everything is – light-setting and camera movements – the better it usually will be. And this was one of the many points Tarkovsky and I agreed on. But looking back, did we really ever disagree about anything?

Andrey encourages, forces us to be receptive to new impressions and go beyond our limitations. This doesn't apply only to us who made the film with him, it also applies to you who will be going to see it.

1986

Source: Brochure issued by the Swedish Film Institute, Motala: Borgströms Tryckeri, 1986.

ERLAND JOSEPHSON

Tarkovsky was as deeply devoted to art as Bergman. For artists of this kind, no scene or detail is unimportant. That is why for me it is almost a crime to show Tarkovsky's films on television. They were created for the big screen, and they contain hardly any close-ups. With Bergman performances had to conform to the accepted conventions of acting, i.e. to aim to present as many of a character's fundamental features and qualities as possible, so the audience is given maximum information. For Tarkovsky, by contrast, the most important thing was for the character to retain an aura of mystery. 'Humans are full of secrets,' he once told me. The difficulty for an actor therefore lay in the need to leave the audience with a degree of uncertainty about the character's thoughts and feelings. Tarkovsky always insisted that a performer should never reveal everything. I have never in all my life known a director who demanded so much work from his audience.

His films are full of long takes, and each episode is a story within a story – an independent tale. For most spectators, used to the logic of conventional viewing, Tarkovsky's films are difficult. And so they need to be seen two or even three times. He was scrupulously careful in his choice of locations, and put a particular emphasis on atmosphere, which he always succeeded in creating. But of course it isn't easy to feel a great deal and reproduce very little of what you feel. I always knew if my acting was going too far by the tone of his voice: 'That's far too brilliant! Exaggeratedly talented!' There was a wonderful naivety about Andrey, and people loved him for it. He saw everything through the eye of his camera. He was always completely open with me, and he never hid his intentions. He never resorted to what Bergman calls 'pedagogical pressure'. And I must confess that I like it when people trust me. Andrey was a man who expressed himself through work, not words. He didn't explain his ideas. If someone looked for a hidden meaning in the fountain in *Nostalgia*, he would just say, 'Water is water'. As far as his work was concerned, he identified with the statement: 'I just want to tell a story.'

We tend to be circumspect with fundamental terms like 'love' and 'death'. We're afraid to trivialize. And so how wonderful it was to meet a man who spoke about them straightforwardly and openly. In this, Andrey was different from the rest of us. It was new to us – or perhaps something we had long since forgotten.

Andrey was pessimistic about the possibility of any complete mutual understanding, any real communication. He said, 'Anyone who has not read Pushkin from childhood onwards will never understand the Russians.' His optimistic cinematic messages contradicted his personal attitudes. For me that is a delightful paradox.

1989

Source: *Izvestia*, 5 April 1989.

INGMAR BERGMAN

My discovery of Tarkovsky's first film was like a miracle.

Suddenly, I found myself standing at the door of a room the keys of which had, until then, never been given to me. It was a room I had always wanted to enter and where he was moving freely and fully at ease.

I felt encouraged and stimulated: someone was expressing what I had always wanted to say without knowing how.

Tarkovsky is for me the greatest, the one who invented a new language, true to the nature of film, as it captures life as a reflection, life as a dream.

1986

Source: Brochure issued by the Swedish Film Institute, Motala: Borgströms Tryckeri, 1986.

CHINGIZ AITMATOV

I feel I must share the strong impression made on me by Andrey Tarkovsky's film *Mirror*. I would just like to touch on one aspect, which for me was the most interesting. An amazingly consistent artist, Tarkovsky is, I believe, most organically connected to that contemporary prose writing that aims to discuss man in the context of a merging of past and present, in an attempt to reflect visually splashes of his emotional memory, splashes of his imagination and multi-layered perceptions of a world that does not always coincide with the reality around us. For me, Tarkovsky's work, both in *Ivan's Childhood* and particularly in *Solaris* and *Mirror*, shows an obvious link to the contemporary literary process, which frequently sacrifices the outer logic of events, phenomena and the actions of its heroes for the sake of an in-depth penetration into their essence.

...For some reason we often equate a non-traditional approach with complexity of form, and sometimes we just combine the two concepts. I believe that in actual fact this is far from true. The reason we do it is presumably that the non-traditional way initially appears unfamiliar and is not immediately accessible, although fundamentally it may be simple, clear and harmonious...

In my view, Andrey Tarkovsky's *Mirror* can be taken as the closest example of this. The dominant idea of the film is that of the difficult fate of kindness, which does not exist in ideal conditions created especially for it, as it were. In real life, kindness constantly runs up against resistance from reality, it seeks out the inner strength to deal with that resistance and continues on its way. In my view, this idea crops up in the film's opening sequences, gradually gathering strength and finally crystallizing in the finale. Tarkovsky talks about this boldly with the audience, convinced of the commonality of his and our moral position, the commonality of his and our spiritual experience.

I therefore believe that the serious, intelligent and thoughtful viewers of today (the only audience of any true artist) will no longer accept direct didacticism and moralizing. They expect films to provide reflection, not simple formulas.

1975

Source: *Sovetskii Ekran*, Moscow, 1975, no. 6, p. 2.
Also published in *Iskusstvo Kino*, Moscow, 1975, no. 6.

ALEKSANDR SOKUROV
The Banal Egalitarianism of Death

Everything was quiet in the ward, but I sensed that no one was asleep. It was all quiet outside the window too, where snow lay in deep piles. There was a terrible Russian frost that year, 1986. The Russians are used to the cold and to deprivation, and they are a patient people. But the cold frosty days never ceased. Every day began with alarming forecasts and figures: minus forty degrees again. 1986 was drawing to a close, and the New Year's celebrations lay ahead, but my fellow-sufferers were sad and depressed. What pleasure can you expect from a holiday spent in hospital? Beside the window was a neon light that bathed the ward in a bluish glow. The man in the next bed, who had a broken arm – a powerful, black-haired fellow with a Ukrainian accent – turned over on his side with a groan so I could see his face and his flashing eyes. He smiled at me, but didn't say a word.

My little transistor radio struggled to find something articulate in the Babel of languages flying through the ether. I tried in vain to capture the sounds of violins or piano. In the ether, chaos ruled. Europe was celebrating

Christmas on all wavelengths. Everything mingled together: the creaking of the sick beds, anonymous cries from the next ward, the nurses' voices and the staccato click of their heels, the rattle of syringes and needles in their metal containers. An almost imperceptible movement on the radio dial, and a man is speaking Russian, with an accent. Short wave. Self-assured, matter-of-fact intonation. Precise, concrete information. 'In Paris... death of...Andrey Tarkovsky...' At that moment I thought I was going to die myself. The next morning the doctor asked me what happened. I answered that Tarkovsky had died. 'So, what has that got to do with you?' the doctor asked. 'Was he a relative of yours?' 'No,' I replied.

...I left the ward and went down to the dark foyer. Huddled under the staircase, I cried for several hours. To be more precise, it wasn't me crying, but something deep inside me. The tears poured out of me, and I started to have difficulty breathing. During all those hours I could not think of anything at all. My insides were churning, as if I were confronting some agonizing moral dilemma, or as if Satan had hurled himself upon me in a destructive rage. What did it all mean? At the time I did not understand it. Sometimes I began to doubt the truth of what I had heard, because there had often been rumours of HIS DEATH. But never before had I had such a strong intuitive belief in the reality of the event as I had that night. But who exactly was I weeping for? Or rather what was I weeping for? HIM? HIM.

Myself!!!?

Myself.

When I'm asked whether I am his student, I always answer no, three times. I have never studied under him, I have never worshipped him. And I will never continue his work, because as artists we must all follow our own paths. The path HE followed, only HE could take. He had discovered his own forest, carved out his own clearing and used his own compass to head NORTH – towards his death. In that there is nothing special. Everyone goes his own way in Russia, or at least everyone who has FAITH in himself does.

In their souls, all Russians are people 'who fight their way through the forests'. Some out of choice, some against their will. Each of us fights through life as if we were fighting through the taiga, making terrible sacrifices along the way. And if it happens that we come across a bright clearing filled with sunshine, berries and soft grass, then of course we lose our heads, we give up the PROMISED LAND to search for new thickets, for new tests in the deadly depths of the forest, never to return to the place where we chanced upon that seductively simple human happiness. Russia – the land of INSPIRATION and ENLIGHTENMENT. Europe – the domain of the intellect. Russia is the place where everything and everyone is to be pitied, where everything and everyone needs help, where many of us can easily awaken in ourselves tender feelings of sentimental romanticism. The Russian finds it hard to hide his self-esteem, which is the most important facet of his nature. This inability to control himself is not aggressive tactlessness, but is part of the national character (but does the nation still exist?).

The Russian has nothing to share – he never had anything and he never will. The Russian is poor – he keeps his money in a sieve full of holes. Materially, the old Russians always lived from one day to the next – that was their shopkeeper spirit. But the SOUL searched for eternal SUCCOUR in the transparent, weightless heavens. But who is this SUCCOUR – GOD, the GENIUS, the REVOLUTIONARY?

We drove in a freezing Zhiguli through the streets of Leningrad. HE sat in the front next to the driver. I can't remember what he was wearing. I only remember that HE was dressed somewhat unusually, and at the time I thought that only HE could dress like that. What did HE have on? I can't remember. And what would that matter now? Yet how could I forget what HE was wearing?...We went into the entrance porch of the cathedral. They were expecting us. The sexton was friendly. Apparently he knew the name Tarkovsky, and offered us his services.

'These are the tombs of the tsars,' he began, 'and there are the tracks of the barbarians. You see – there, and there. Here the bronze monogram is missing, and here some visitor has pursued his "art" by tearing the heads off the two-headed eagle on the memorial slab.'

'Why do they do such things?' asked Tarkovsky.

'They use them as models to make bronze copies of the imperial coat-of-arms that they can get rid of on the black market. It's something that sells. It's popular,' the sexton said. 'But it's not just a Russian phenomenon. You'll find these thieves in museums all over the world,' he added, in the tone of a man who has travelled the globe and wishes to defend the FATHERLAND.

Then he took us to the inner sanctum of the cathedral, where we found ourselves standing before the dusty remains of an old carriage. It made a sombre impression. We said nothing. 'In this carriage, Russian revolutionaries murdered Tsar Aleksandr II, which people rather regret nowadays. He was a democrat, that tsar, but they murdered him all the same, and threw their bombs all the same. Since then, what was left of his carriage has remained here. People say that at the time you could see the tsar's bloodstains on the doors and the silk of the seat...'

It was cold in the cathedral, and our shoes left fleeting wet marks on the cold memorial slabs. There was not a speck of dust on these polished marble stones – nothing but the reflection of a distant winter sunbeam. We climbed up the ever narrowing spire via a cast-iron spiral staircase – if my memory serves me correctly – that brought us to a little window with red copper fittings. The two of us pushed hard on the frame, which finally gave a loud creak and opened outwards. Below us lay frost-bitten Leningrad. This year, too, it was an icy winter, and we could see for miles. We could have lost ourselves in never-ending contemplation of what lay before our eyes. Perhaps for the rest of our lives. But it was much too cold. Tarkovsky gazed in silence over the freezing city for as long as he was able. I noticed he was not at all frightened by the fact that we were almost a hundred metres up. And that his face showed no emotion – one might have thought he had been here several times before and today was merely fulfilling his obligation to follow his host. I felt put out, and could not hide my irritation. I had gone to so much trouble to impress my 'guest from Moscow' with this unique view, and I had promised myself the reward of his unconditional admiration.

But the 'guest from Moscow' just went on looking out into space, without revealing any sign of his feelings. Until the end of my days I shall never forget this view of the Europeanized Russian city. And I shall never forget what HE said to me in the car, when HE had warmed himself up: 'I grew calm once I realized that fate had chosen me. There was a temptation, which of course I resisted. After that, I relied on fate and did what fate told me to do.'

...A black, broad-brimmed hat, a plain black coat, a little too long. Some dandy came shimmying across the hotel lobby. An over-dressed man who attracted everyone's attention. We were standing on the other side, waiting for Tarkovsky. A grey winter's morning in Leningrad – and even the hotel foyer was in semi-darkness. A dozy, bad-tempered porter and the smell of freshly brewed coffee. They were expecting us at Leningrad University, and we were already a little late. The dandy paced up and down by the newspaper stand, and when the light of an old bronze chandelier caught him, we could see that for some reason he was smiling.

...He is a madman. His films are just self-promotion. He is arrogant. Nothing he does is of any use to the Soviet people. He aspires to transcendency. He is completely crazy. Everything comes out stilted. All just shadows, no characters. Rhetorical phrases, declarations shovelled into the mouths of abused actors. Pseudo philosophy. 'Those who believe in him should call him to order, should show him his place' – those were more or less the thoughts of the famous Soviet film director Marlen Khutsiev on *Mirror*. It's a terrible thing when even colleagues who themselves have suffered under totalitarian pressure and violence turn on the creator of *Mirror* and tear him to shreds. Then, as now, there were many who did not understand HIS rigorous determination.

A god? A genius? A revolutionary?

A Russian.

What a disaster it is for modern man to undergo humiliation and suffering brought about by violence! If this is what society forces its artists, teachers and doctors to experience, then it will have to bear the evil consequences: people will take the wrong side; the neurotic and pathological, lies and *nostalgie de la boue* will flourish. Tarkovsky and his talent were envied by his contemporaries, and this envy was deep-rooted and deadly. It was envy of the kind the castrated feel towards the potent. And it was all too easy to grow indignant about Tarkovsky: with envious anger the 'state' defended the 'honest' indignation of those who represented the interests and morality of the 'entire Soviet people'. And the indignation and hostility grew as this GREAT ARTIST fulfilled his messianic role. Hour after hour, year after year, the state and the people refused him the right to speak with his own voice. In a life shaped by ideology, it was not possible to walk upright, and humane thought became the enemy. Aesthetic ideas were curtailed by political sloganeering that drew fantastic conclusions from what in effect was still unknown. But the political aspect of this situation should not distract our attention from a considerably older problem – that of film as ART...

I should phrase the question more precisely: is film in its modern form an *independent* art at all? My own reflections have convinced me that the modern film cannot yet assume the responsibilities of an adult. The modern film is a suckling, whose sex, whose affiliation to some form, genre or class of the living world is as yet undetermined. What is clear is that the disastrous dependence of cinema on literature, the dramatic arts, theatre and fine art is demoralizing for the film-maker. In international cinema people boast of a 'film basket' – a cinema that integrates and combines all the arts! But there is no guarantee that anything new will come out of such an amalgamation.

Nevertheless, the great contemporary directors have discovered and to a certain degree developed a single cinematically artistic (!) quality: TIME. The passage of time is the most important subject of analysis within their profession. And while Her Majesty TIME remains heavily dependent on dramaturgy in the films of Bergman and Antonioni, there is a specifically cinematographical time in Tarkovsky and Bresson, which is created by visual means and so can exist only as cinematographical reality. It can be neither described nor reproduced in any other medium. Tarkovsky was undoubtedly engaged in the battle to create a 'real' film, and the unique quality of this 'real film' lay in the individual reception of a largely individual viewpoint and mode of expression on the part of the auteur. Try to imagine how many film-makers could produce such work. Very few. For the rest of us, the only alternatives are to destroy these pioneers or to come to terms with their achievement and then take over their allotted places. But in that case one should not speak of art, because it is design which rules – everything that conforms to customs and conventions, that makes life more comfortable.

Although Tarkovsky did not develop any practical means of fighting his opponents, the very fact of his existence posed a major threat to those of his colleagues who were also his fellow-countrymen. They were unable to accept what he had achieved and were even more afraid of what HE might come up with in the future. In the course of time he attracted the attention of the young, and that could have led to his triumph.

The black hat of the DANDY covered the head of a black-haired man who greeted us. It was Tarkovsky. We had not recognized him, whereas he had been observing us the whole time. I have never seen a man so elegantly dressed. I could see the maestro knew how to wear his clothes, that he had distinctive taste and a preference for quality. Then we were sitting in the car again, and as before I could only look at him sideways.

Our meeting with the students at Leningrad University had just ended. The students had immediately showered him with silly questions and had evidently only come to catch a glimpse of this source of scandal, the 'transcendentalist'.

'Cock-eyed,' said Tarkovsky, upset and annoyed as he strode out of the hall. 'The day has got off to a bad start.' He said that when he was in the car, his hat cast to one side, his coat unbuttoned. A wet Leningrad snow was falling. The car had stopped at a traffic light. The noise of the windscreen wipers swishing to and fro, the bright red traffic light. We did not speak. It was hard and painful to look at HIM. It was shameful. One felt ashamed for the FATHERLAND.

This journey to Leningrad was connected with the need to put the financial affairs of HIS family in order. For every appearance he was paid a modest fee, but each was the source of pain and irritation. The audiences often contained neurotics who wanted to have an 'intellectual' go at him, while others brought files or manuscripts and asked him to read them as soon as possible and then tell them when he would 'start shooting'... But there were others, too, who believed in him, who loved him, and who were afraid of saying something that might offend. They gazed at him with adoring eyes and worshipped everything about him – his gestures, voice, clothes. These people represent the bright side of Russian life. They know what it means to cope day after day with chaotic conditions and all the obstacles to a productive life. But they also know the all-important truth: that life revolves around culture and faith, and by comparison everything else comes a poor second. With their hearts they sense who are the best among their fellow-countrymen, and they come to their aid with all the energy contained in those hearts, sacrificing themselves for the CREATOR. No one has a higher regard for the ARTIST than these simple Russian folk. Russia's art is built on them, for them, because of them, and for their sake. The tongues of these people are still, but their eyes send out their prayers. They sit there in silence, announcing their presence only through friendly notes passed from row to row up to the podium. Their faces are suffused with the secret hope that the eyes of the CREATOR might dwell on one of them, just for a moment, for this will light up their souls.

Dear God, how alike people are, and how easy to understand – at least, those who live the same lives as ourselves. In Russia an ARTIST who is not also a prophet is a *nobody*. Only through such a mission can he achieve the longed-for goal of every Russian CREATOR – to be NECESSARY. The strange thing about Russian life is that our people have an ongoing need for prophetic ideas. Russians are accustomed to the fact that someone is always leading them somewhere. We are an extraordinary people, always on the move, which is why we have never really settled, not even when we are at HOME. And if that is how it is, then one of the consequences must be that there are victims along the way... There is no time to stop and help the meek and weak.

...That same evening we walked through the hushed rooms of Pushkin's last apartment. The magnificent suite was bathed in the semi-darkness of a winter's evening. We watched our shadows, cast by the light from the lamps. Nina Popova, who runs the museum, followed, treading softly behind us. Now she lights some candles, and we are standing in front of Pushkin's deathbed. Silence. Tarkovsky smiles. It's true, he smiles. Obviously he is thinking of something completely personal.

'Are there many authentic objects here?' he asks Popova.

'No, unfortunately, only a few...'

There is a picture on the wall. Pushkin in his coffin.

'He wanted this death,' says Tarkovsky. 'You see that smile – he wanted death...'

'Yes, he had lived a full life, he had nothing else to live for,' I agree.

'You could make a wonderful film about Pushkin,' Tarkovsky says to me – again with a smile. That was unexpected. I looked at him.

I remember thinking at the time how very wrong GENIUS can be! I shall never make a film about Pushkin. That cannot be my path. In the life of this Russian, everything is far too understandable, too obvious.

Tarkovsky 'studied' and intuitively understood the museum, which was more like a necropolis. It smelled of a death that followed a terrible battle against life, a fight to reach the void. Tarkovsky looked like a healthy man, but that was only an outer impression. In the morning he drew parallels between his heartbeat and the Leningrad sky. All in all, he was a man closely bound to Nature – a 'child of Nature'. His interest in it was inexhaustible. But what affected me most was his belief that he had supernatural powers. As we were about to leave the 'necropolis', I mentioned that I was beginning to get a headache. Immediately Tarkovsky sat me on a chair and with stroking movements across my head began to create some kind of electric current. I could see this display gave him enormous satisfaction, and so I began to lie – to lie about what this nonsense was achieving. I described how a warmth was spreading...as if certain forces were coming from somewhere...as if everything was beginning to get brighter within me. In short, I described images of a physical and spiritual rebirth...The maestro was happy. Today I regret not having told him the truth. In fact, the headache got worse and worse, and I felt not the slightest warmth from his hands.

No, I did not feel the warmth of his hands. But in those years I did feel with all *my* being the SHADOW of *his* being.

That was truly Russian. Those who loved him canonized him, even during his lifetime. And so it was as if he were living in two different dimensions. To some he was a saint and a genius, and to the rest he was a madman.

One sunny day, Anatoli Solonitsyn came to HIM with a personal problem. I was sitting in a corner of the room, and he didn't notice me. He had come to ask his GOD, the film director now out of favour, for money. No, he didn't actually want to borrow money, but he wanted advice on how to get hold of some. For years the famous and respected Solonitsyn had not been able to afford his own apartment, but now he had been offered a cooperative apartment, and it would cost a lot of money. They sat quietly in the sunlit room and brooded over the banal problem of an apartment. Then Larisa Pavlovna, Tarkovsky's wife, came home from market with some vegetables she had bought. She prepared some meat which, hungry as we were, we wolfed down. The meat was not quite cooked – in other words, it was a bit raw. It was the first time – and I can say with absolute certainty the last – I had eaten anything like it. Strange: I never lost the feeling that I was in a house where there was always abundance, even though Larisa Pavlovna never knew how she would manage to pay all the debts. Her life was free of all Russian and material constraints. Despite the pressure of financial problems, the pride of the genius solved everything.

Tarkovsky is a monument to Russian film art in the second half of the 20th century. But his innovations were actually not his own. Everything he transferred from the material world into the spiritual already existed in one form or another in Russian poetry and philosophy. The conflicts and commonalities of Soviet Russian life were in his blood. But according to his own view of himself, he was above all a European artist. The only personality in Russian cultural history to whom I can draw a parallel is the great Tyutchev, that Russian cosmopolitan and Messiah who was sent to us from the 19th century into the 21st. But there is a difference: Tyutchev was a favourite of the politicians, whereas Tarkovsky was not.

'...Everything here is fine, so please don't worry yourselves – everything's OK...!!!' That was the sort of thing he would say to me over the telephone from Italy. But I could sense that this was no longer his true voice. My subconscious told me we would never meet again. This voice sounded like the dubbed speech of a cartoon character, completely flat and monotonous. I did not believe a single one of those comforting words – not one. And I gave no credence to rumours about his fatal illness, though I often thought about the cruel heartlessness of FATE. Why did it have to expose this Russian martyr to such terrible homesickness? Why did HE have to endure the withering of his own life? 'Hurry up and put your affairs in order,' the doctor told his patient, the film director, when he gave him the diagnosis.

Somewhere high above, where his SOUL is a reality, there is an answer to the question of what POWERS kept this man alive when he was so aware of his own end. If only we could learn how the SOUL feels up there – whether it is calm. Or cold. Or free.

Some music was being played, and then the train left Leningrad. At that time few people recognized his face, so we could go undisturbed to the carriage; no one turned round, no one grasped his elbow. A great Russian, not very tall, with inexhaustible energy, cheerful and grateful for our help with his everyday problems – there he sat with his son Andrey and wife Larisa Pavlovna in the railway compartment. Tarkovsky pulled a small camera from his pocket and pointed it at us. The compartment was in semi-darkness, and only their faces glowed. I never saw those photographs, and so one might wonder if I've only imagined all this. A beautiful vision, is it not?

The train left the station, and once again it began to snow.

We Russians expect it to snow. For a Russian it is very important to know what sort of earth one's coffin is to be placed in. It's true that his grave is not here with us (for which he is not to blame). But we are the only people in the world who share his mental agony – we bear his image and his being.

...They have taken the man in the next bed away to change his bandages. In the ward it's quiet and gloomy. The little fanlights have been opened, and a pitiless cold cuts through our warmth. I pull the bedclothes over my head and try to imagine how they will bury him in the Novodyevichy Cemetery, and who will make a speech.

The death of a GREAT man – that is a fearsome reminder of the fate of all men. Without HIM it was terrible for me. I felt I no longer had anyone to defend me. This man, who had illuminated my whole being with his blessing and his FAITH, *was gone*. And so it was evident that I was nothing but a perfectly ordinary egoist. As I wept for the torments of his life and the agonizing pain of his death, ultimately I was pitying only myself. And yet I also understood that I would remain a man and would take on myself the burden of an orphaned life.

Leningrad/Moscow, July 1987

ANDREY TARKOVSKY

Extracts from *Sculpting in Time*

TRANSLATED BY KITTY HUNTER-BLAIR

THE SPIRITUAL MEANING OF THE ART OF CINEMA

To start with the most general consideration, it is worth saying that the indisputably functional role of art lies in the idea of *knowing*, where the effect is expressed as shock, as catharsis.

From the very moment when Eve ate the apple from the tree of knowledge, mankind was doomed to strive endlessly after the truth. First, as we know, Adam and Eve discovered they were naked. And they were ashamed. They were ashamed because they had understood; and then they set out on their way in the joy of knowing one another. That was the beginning of a journey that has no end. One can understand how dramatic that moment was for those two souls, just emerged from the state of placid ignorance and thrown out into the vastness of the earth, hostile and inexplicable.

'With the sweat of thy brow shalt thou earn thy bread...'

So it was that man, 'nature's crown', arrived on the earth in order to *know* why it was that he had appeared or been sent.

And with man's help the Creator comes to know himself. This progress has been given the name of evolution, and it is accompanied by the agonizing process of human self-knowledge.

In a very real sense every individual experiences this process for himself as he comes to know life, himself, his aims. Of course each person uses the sum of knowledge accumulated by humanity, but all the same the experience of ethical, moral self-knowledge is the only aim in life for each person, and, subjectively, it is experienced each time as something new. Again and again man correlates himself with the world, racked with longing to acquire, and become one with, the ideal which lies outside him, which he apprehends as some kind of intuitively sensed first principle. The unattainability of that becoming one, the inadequacy of his own 'I', is the perpetual source of man's dissatisfaction and pain.

And so art, like science, is a means of assimilating the world, an instrument for knowing it in the course of man's journey towards what is called 'absolute truth'.

That, however, is the end of any similarity between these two embodiments of the creative human spirit, in which man does not merely discover, but creates. For the moment it is far more important to note the divergence, the difference in principle, between the two forms of knowing: scientific and aesthetic.

By means of art man takes over reality through a subjective experience. In science man's knowledge of the world makes its way up an endless staircase and is successively replaced by new knowledge, with one discovery often enough being disproved by the next for the sake of a particular objective truth. An artistic discovery occurs each time as a new and unique image of the world, a hieroglyphic of absolute truth. It appears as a revelation, as a momentary, passionate wish to grasp intuitively and at a stroke *all* the laws of this world – its beauty and ugliness, its compassion and cruelty, its infinity and its limitations. The artist expresses these things by creating the image, *sui generis* detector of the absolute. Through the image is sustained an awareness of the infinite: the eternal within the finite, the spiritual within matter, the limitless given form.

Art could be said to be a symbol of the universe, being linked with that absolute spiritual truth which is hidden from us in our positivistic, pragmatic activities. [pp. 36–37]

Art is born and takes hold wherever there is a timeless and insatiable longing for the spiritual, for the ideal: that longing which draws people to art. Modern art has taken a wrong turn in abandoning the search for the meaning of existence in order to affirm the value of the individual for its own sake. What purports to be art begins to look like an eccentric occupation for suspect characters who maintain that any personalized action is of intrinsic value simply as a display of self-will. But in artistic creation the personality does not assert itself, it serves another, higher and communal idea. The artist is always a servant, and is perpetually trying to pay for the gift that has been given to him as if by a miracle. Modern man, however, does not want to make any sacrifice, even though true affirmation of self can only be expressed in sacrifice. We are gradually forgetting about this, and at the same time, inevitably, losing all sense of our human calling....

When I speak of the aspiration towards the beautiful, of the ideal as the ultimate aim of art, which grows from a yearning for that ideal, I am not for a moment suggesting that art should shun the 'dirt' of the world. On the contrary! The artistic image is always a metonym, where one thing is substituted for another, the smaller for the greater. To tell of what is living, the artist uses something dead; to speak of the infinite, he shows the finite. Substitution...the infinite cannot be made into matter, but it is possible to create an illusion of the infinite: the image. [p. 38]

An image can be created and make itself felt. It may be accepted or rejected. But none of this can be understood in any cerebral sense. The idea of infinity cannot be expressed in words or even described, but it can be apprehended through art, which makes infinity tangible. The absolute is only attainable through faith and in the creative act.

The only condition of fighting for the right to create is faith in your own vocation, readiness to serve, and refusal to compromise. Artistic creation demands of the artist that he 'perish utterly', in the full, tragic sense of those words. And so, if art carries within it a hieroglyphic of absolute truth, this will always be an image of the world, made manifest in the work once and for all time. And if cold, positivistic, scientific cognition of the world is like the ascent of an unending staircase, its artistic counterpoint suggests an endless system of spheres, each one perfect and contained within itself. One may complement or contradict another, but in no circumstances can they cancel each other out; on the contrary, they enrich one another, and accumulate to form an all-embracing sphere that grows out into infinity. These poetic revelations, each one valid and eternal, are evidence of man's capacity to recognize in whose image and likeness he is made, and to voice this recognition.

Moreover, the great function of art is communication, since mutual understanding is a force to unite people, and the spirit of communion is one of the most important aspects of artistic creativity. Works of art, unlike those of science, have no practical goals in any material sense. Art is a meta-language, with the help of which people try to communicate with one another; to impart information about themselves and assimilate the experience of others. Again, this has to do not with practical advantage but with realizing the idea of love, the meaning of which is in sacrifice: the very antithesis of pragmatism. I simply cannot believe that an artist can ever work only for the sake of 'self-expression'. Self-expression is meaningless unless it meets with a response. For the sake of creating a spiritual bond with others it can only be an agonizing process, one that involves no practical gain: ultimately, it is an act of sacrifice. But surely it cannot be worth the effort merely for the sake of hearing one's own echo? [pp. 38–40]

In creating an image [the artist] subordinates his own thought, which becomes insignificant in the face of that emotionally perceived image of the world that has appeared to him like a revelation. For thought is brief, whereas the image is absolute. In the case of someone who is spiritually receptive, it is therefore possible to talk of an analogy between the impact made by a work of art and that of a purely religious experience. Art acts above all on the soul, shaping its spiritual structure.

A poet has the imagination and psychology of a child, for his impressions of the world are immediate, however profound his ideas about the world may be. Of course one may say of a child, too, that he is a philosopher, but only in some very relative sense. And art flies in the face of philosophical concepts. The poet does not use 'descriptions' of the world; he himself has a hand in its creation.

Only when a person is willing and able to trust the artist, to believe him, can he be sensitive and susceptible to art. But how hard it sometimes is to cross the threshold of incomprehension which cuts us off from the emotional, poetic image. In just the same way, for a true faith in God, or even in order to feel a need for that faith, a person has to have a certain cast of soul, a particular spiritual potentiality. [pp. 41–42]

The meaning of religious truth is *hope*. Philosophy seeks the truth, defining the meaning of human activity, the limits of human reason, the meaning of existence, even when the philosopher reaches the conclusion that existence is senseless, and human effort – futile.

The allotted function of art is not, as is often assumed, to put across ideas, to propagate thoughts, to serve as example. The aim of art is to prepare a person for death, to plough and harrow his soul, rendering it capable of turning to good. [p. 43]

I want to underline my own belief that art must carry man's craving for the ideal, must be an expression of his reaching out towards it; that art must give man hope and faith. And the more hopeless the world in the artist's version, the more clearly perhaps must we see the ideal that stands in opposition to it – otherwise life becomes impossible!

Art symbolizes the meaning of our existence. [p. 192]
I see it as my duty to stimulate reflection on what is essentially human and eternal in each individual soul, and which all too often a person will pass by, even though his fate lies in his hands. He is too busy chasing after phantoms and bowing down to idols. In the end everything can be reduced to the one simple element which is all a person can count upon in his existence: the capacity to love. That element can grow within the soul to become the supreme factor which determines the meaning of a person's life. [p. 200]

THE SPIRITUAL POETRY OF FILM IMAGES

There are some aspects of human life that can only be faithfully represented through poetry. But this is where directors very often try to use clumsy, conventional gimmickry instead of poetic logic. I'm thinking of the illusionism and extraordinary effects involved in dreams, memories and fantasies. All too often film dreams are made into a collection of old-fashioned filmic tricks, and cease to be a phenomenon of life.

Faced with the necessity of shooting dreams, we had to decide how to come close to the particular poetry of the dream, how to express it, what means to use. This was not something that could be decided in the abstract. Casting around for an answer we tried out several practical possibilities, using associations and vague guesses. Quite unexpectedly it occurred to us to have negative images in the third dream. In our mind's eye we glimpsed black sunlight sparkling through snowy trees and a downpour of gleaming rain. Flashes of lightning came in to make it technically feasible to cut from positive to negative. But all this merely created an atmosphere of unreality. What about the content? What about the logic of the dream? That came from memories. I remembered seeing the wet grass, the lorry load of apples, the horses, wet with rain, steaming in the sunshine. All this material found its way into the film straight from life, not through the medium of contiguous visual arts. Looking for simple solutions to the problem of conveying the unreality of the dream we hit on the panorama of moving trees in negative, and, against that background, the face of the little girl passing in front of the camera three times, her expression changed with each appearance. We wanted to capture in that scene the child's foreboding of imminent tragedy. The last scene of the dream was deliberately shot near water, on the beach, in order to link it with the last dream of Ivan. [pp. 30–31]

Of late I have frequently found myself addressing audiences, and I have noticed that whenever I declare that there are no symbols or metaphors in my films, those present express incredulity. They persist in asking again and again, for instance, what rain signifies in my films; why does it figure in film after film; and why the repeated images of wind, fire, water? I really don't know how to deal with such questions. Rain is after all typical of the landscape in which I grew up; in Russia you have those long, dreary, persistent rains. And I can say that I love nature – I don't like big cities and feel perfectly happy when I'm away from the paraphernalia of modern civilisation, just as I felt wonderful in Russia when I was in my country house, with three hundred kilometres between Moscow and myself. Rain, fire, water, snow, dew, the driving ground wind – all are part of the material setting in which we dwell; I would even say of the truth of our lives. I am therefore puzzled when I am told that people cannot simply enjoy watching nature, when it is lovingly reproduced on the screen, but have to look for some hidden meaning they feel it must contain. Of course rain can just be seen as bad weather, whereas I use it to create a particular aesthetic setting in which to steep the action of the film. But that is not at all the same thing as bringing nature into my films as a symbol of something else – Heaven forbid! In commercial cinema nature often does not exist at all; all one has is the most advantageous lighting and interiors for the purpose of quick shooting – everybody follows the plot and no one is bothered by the artificiality of a setting that is more or less right, nor by the disregard for detail and atmosphere. When the screen brings the real world to the audience, the world as it actually is, so that it can be seen in depth and from all sides, evoking its very 'smell', allowing audiences to feel on their skin its moisture or its dryness – it seems that the cinema-goer has so lost the capacity simply to surrender to an immediate, emotional aesthetic impression, that he instantly has to check himself, and ask: 'Why? What for? What's the point?' The answer is that I want to create my own world on the screen, in its ideal and most perfect form, as I myself feel it and see it. I am not trying to be coy with my audience, or to conceal some secret intention of my own: I am recreating my world in those details which seem to me most fully and exactly to express the elusive meaning of our existence. [pp. 212–13]

People have often asked me what the Zone is, and what it symbolizes, and have put forward wild conjectures on the subject. I'm reduced to a state of fury and despair by such questions. The Zone doesn't symbolize anything, any more than anything else does in my films: the zone is a zone. [p. 200]

The image is indivisible and elusive, dependent upon our consciousness and on the real world which it seeks to embody. If the world is inscrutable, then the image will be so too. It is a kind of equation, signifying the correlation between truth and the human consciousness, bound as the latter is by Euclidean space. We cannot comprehend the totality of the universe, but the poetic image is able to express that totality. The image is an impression of the truth, a glimpse of the truth permitted to us in our blindness.

The incarnate image will be faithful when its articulations are palpably the expression of truth, when they make it unique, singular – as life itself is, even in its simplest manifestations. [p. 106]

THE SPIRITUAL POETRY OF SOUNDS

I should like to hope that [music] has never been a flat illustration of what was happening on the screen, to be felt as a kind of emotional aura around the objects shown, in order to force the audience to see the image in the way I wanted. In every instance, music in cinema is for me a natural part of our resonant world, a part of human life. Nevertheless, it is quite possible that in a sound film that is realized with complete theoretical consistency, there will be no place for music: it will be replaced by sounds in which cinema constantly discovers new levels of meaning. That is what I was aiming at in *Stalker* and *Nostalgia*.

It may be that in order to make the cinematic image sound authentically, in its full diapason, music has to be abandoned. For strictly speaking the world as transformed by cinema and the world as transformed by music are parallel, and conflict with each other. Properly organized in a film, the resonant world is musical in its essence – and that is the true music of cinema. [p. 159]

Above all, I feel that the sounds of this world are so beautiful in themselves that if only we could learn to listen to them properly, cinema would have no need of music at all.

Nonetheless, there are moments in modern cinema when music is exploited with consummate mastery. [p. 162]

Electronic music seems to me to have enormously rich possibilities for cinema. Artemiev and I used it in some scenes in *Mirror*.

We wanted the sound to be close to that of an earthly echo, filled with poetic suggestion – to rustling, to sighing. The notes had to convey the fact that reality is conditional, and at the same time accurately to reproduce precise states of mind, the sounds of a person's interior world. The moment we hear what it is, and realise that it's being constructed, electronic music dies; and Artemiev had to use very complex devices to achieve the sounds we wanted. Electronic music must be purged of its 'chemical' origins, so that as we listen we may catch in it the primary notes of the world.

Instrumental music is artistically so autonomous that it is far harder for it to dissolve into the film to the point where it becomes an organic part of it. Therefore its use will always involve some measure of compromise, because it is always illustrative. Furthermore, electronic music has exactly that capacity for being absorbed into the sound. It can be hidden behind other noises and remain indistinct; like the voice of nature, of vague intimations...It can be like somebody breathing. [pp. 162–63]

TIME REAL AND REMEMBERED

Time is a condition for the existence of our 'I'. It is like a kind of culture medium that is destroyed when it is no longer needed, once the links are severed between the individual personality and the conditions of existence. And the moment of death is also the death of individual time: the life of a human being becomes inaccessible to the feelings of those remaining alive, dead for those around him.

Time is necessary to man, so that, made flesh, he may be able to realize himself as a personality. But I am not thinking of linear time, meaning the possibility of getting something done, performing some action. The action is a result, and what I am considering is the cause which makes man incarnate in a moral sense.

History is still not Time; nor is evolution. They are both consequences. Time is a state: the flame in which there lives the salamander of the human soul.

Time and memory merge into each other; they are like the two sides of a medal. It is obvious enough that without Time, memory cannot exist either. But memory is something so complex that no list of all its attributes could define the totality of the impressions through which it affects us. Memory is a spiritual concept! For instance, if somebody tells us of his impressions of childhood, we can say with certainty that we shall have enough material in our hands to form a complete picture of that person. Bereft of memory, a person becomes the prisoner of an illusory existence; falling out of time he is unable to seize his own link with the outside world – in other words he is doomed to madness. [pp. 57–58]

Time is said to be irreversible. And this is true enough in the sense that 'you can't bring back the past', as they say. But what exactly is this 'past'? Is it what has passed? And what does 'passed' mean for a person when for each of us the past is the bearer of all that is constant in the reality of the present, of each current moment? In a certain sense the past is far more real, or at any rate more stable, more resilient than the present. The present slips and vanishes like sand between the fingers, acquiring material weight only in its recollection. King Solomon's rings bore the inscription, 'All will pass'; by contrast, I want to draw attention to how time in its moral implication is in fact turned back. Time cannot vanish without trace for it is a subjective, spiritual category; and the time we have lived settles in our soul as an experience placed within time. [p. 58]

In his account of Japan, the Soviet journalist Vsevolod Ovchinnikov wrote: 'It is considered that time, *per se*, helps to make known the essence of things. The Japanese therefore see a particular charm in the evidence of old age. They are attracted to the darkened tone of an old tree, the ruggedness of a stone, or even the scruffy look of a picture whose edges have been handled by a great many people. To all these signs of age they give the name, *saba*, which literally means "rust". *Saba*, then, is a natural rustiness, the charm of olden days, the stamp of time. [– or patina – *A.T.*]

'*Saba*, as an element of beauty, embodies the link between art and nature.'

In a sense the Japanese could be said to be trying to master time as the stuff of art. [p. 59]

What is the essence of the director's work? We could define it as sculpting in time. Just as a sculptor takes a lump of marble, and, inwardly conscious of the features of his finished piece, removes everything that is not part of it – so the film-maker, from a 'lump of time' made up of an enormous, solid cluster of living facts, cuts off and discards whatever he does not need, leaving only what is to be an element of the finished film, what will prove to be integral to the cinematic image. [pp. 63–64]

Time in the form of fact: again I come back to it. I see chronicle as the ultimate cinema; for me it is not a way of filming but a way of reconstructing, of recreating life. [pp. 64–65]

This is how I conceive an ideal piece of filming: the author takes millions of metres of film, on which systematically, second by second, day by day and year by year, a man's life, for instance, from birth to death, is followed and recorded, and out of all that come two and a half thousand metres, or an hour and a half of screen time. (It is curious also to imagine those millions of metres going through the hands of several directors for each to make his film – how different they would all be!) [p. 65]

The cinema image, then, is basically observation of life's facts within time, organized according to the pattern of life itself, and observing its time laws. Observations are selective: we leave on film only what is justified as integral to the image. Not that the cinematic image can be divided and segmented against its time-nature, current time cannot be removed from it. The image becomes authentically cinematic when (amongst other things) not only does it live within time, but time also lives within it, even within each separate frame. [p. 68]

It is above all through sense of time, through rhythm, that the director reveals his individuality. Rhythm colours a work with stylistic marks. It is not thought up, not composed on an arbitrary, theoretical basis, but comes into being spontaneously in a film, in response to the director's innate awareness of life, his 'search for time'. It seems to me that time in a shot has to flow independently and with dignity, then ideas will find their place in it without fuss, bustle, haste. [p. 120]

I see it as my professional task then, to create my own, distinctive flow of time, and convey in the shot a sense of its movement – from lazy and soporific to stormy and swift – and to one person it will seem one way, to another, another. [pp. 120–21]

Rhythm, then, is not the metrical sequence of pieces; what makes it is time-thrust within the frames. And I am convinced that it is rhythm, and not editing, as people tend to think, that is the main formative element of cinema. [p. 119]

The dominant, all-powerful factor of the film image is *rhythm*, expressing the course of time within the frame.

The actual passage of time is also made clear in the characters' behaviour, the visual treatment and the sound – but these are all accompanying features, the absence of which, theoretically, would in no way affect the existence of the film. One cannot conceive of a cinematic work with no sense of time passing through the shot, but one can easily imagine a film with no actors, music, décor or even editing. [p. 113]

THE FILM ACTOR

It can sometimes be a grave drawback for the actor to know the director's plan too well at the start of shooting. It is for the director to build up the role, thus giving the actor total freedom in each separate section – a freedom that cannot happen in theatre. If the film actor constructs his own role, he loses the opportunity for spontaneous and involuntary playing within the terms laid down by the plan and purpose of the film. The director has to induce the right state of mind in him, and then make sure that it is constantly sustained. And the actor can be brought to the right state of mind by various mean – it depends upon the circumstances of the set, and on the personality of the actor with whom you are working. The latter has to be in a psychological state that is impossible to feign. No one who is downhearted can hide the fact completely – and what cinema demands is the truth of a state of mind that cannot be concealed. [p. 139]

When I am making a film I try not to wear down the actors with discussion, and am adamant that the actor should not connect any pieces he plays with the whole, sometimes not even to his own immediately preceding and following scenes. [p. 140]

THE CRISIS OF MODERN CIVILIZATION

Indeed, in the art of the latter half of the twentieth century, mystery has been lost. Today artists want instantaneous and total recognition – immediate payment for something that takes place in the realm of the spirit. In this respect the figure of Kafka is outstanding: he printed nothing during his lifetime, and in his will instructed his executor to burn all he had written; in mentality he belonged, morally speaking, to the past. That was why he suffered so much, being out of tune with his time.

What passes for art today is for the most part fiction, for it is a fallacy to suppose that method can become the meaning and aim of art. Nonetheless, most modern artists spend their time self-indulgently demonstrating method.

The whole question of *avant-garde* is peculiar to the twentieth century, to the time when art has steadily been losing its spirituality. The situation is worst in the visual arts, which today are almost totally devoid of spirituality. The accepted view is that this situation reflects the despiritualized state of society. And of course, on the level of simple observation of the tragedy, I agree: that is what it does reflect. But art must transcend as well as observe; its role is to bring spiritual vision to bear on reality: as did Dostoyevsky, the first to have given inspired utterance to the incipient disease of the age.

The whole concept of *avant-garde* in art is meaningless. I can see what it means as applied to sport, for instance. But to apply it to art would be to accept the idea of progress in art; and though progress has an obvious place in technology – more perfect machines, capable of carrying out their functions better and more accurately – how can anyone be more advanced in art? How could Thomas Mann be said to be better than Shakespeare?

People tend to talk about experiment and search above all in relation to the *avant-garde*. But what does it mean? How can you experiment in art? Have a go and see how it turns out? But if it hasn't worked, then there's nothing to see except the private problem of the person who has failed. For the work of art carries within it an integral aesthetic and philosophical unity; it is an organism, living and developing according to its own laws. Can one talk of experiment in relation to the birth of a child? It is senseless and immoral. [pp. 96–97]

Throughout the history of civilization, the historical process has essentially consisted of the 'right' way, the 'correct' way – a better one every time – conceived in the minds of the ideologues and politicians, being offered to people for the salvation of the world and the improvement of man's position within it. In order to be part of this process of reorganization, 'the few' had each time to waive their own way of thinking and direct their efforts outside themselves to fit in with the proposed plan of action. Thus involved in dynamic outward activity for the sake of a 'progress' that would save the future and mankind, the individual forgot about all that was specifically, personally, and essentially his own; caught up in the general effort he came to underestimate the significance of his own spiritual nature, and the result has been an ever more irreconcilable conflict between the individual and society. Concerned for the interests of the many, nobody thought of his own in the sense preached by Christ: 'Love your neighbour as yourself.' That is, love yourself so much that you respect in yourself the supra-personal, divine principle, which forbids you to pursue your acquisitive, selfish interests and tells you to give yourself, without reasoning or talking about it; to love others. This requires a true sense of your own dignity: an acceptance of the objective value and significance of the 'I' at the centre of your life on earth, as it grows in spiritual stature, advancing towards the perfection in which there can be no egocentricity. In the fight for your own soul, fidelity to yourself demands unceasing, single-minded effort. It is so much easier to slip down than it is to rise one iota above your own narrow, opportunistic motives. [p. 232]

It is obvious to everyone that man's material aggrandisement has not been synchronous with spiritual progress. The point has been reached where we seem to have a fatal incapacity for mastering our material achievements in order to use them for our own good. We have created a civilization which threatens to annihilate mankind.

In the face of disaster on that global scale, the one issue that has to be raised, it seems to me, is the question of a man's personal responsibility, and his willingness for sacrifice, without which he ceases to be a spiritual being in any real sense. [p. 234]

Today, civilized society, the great majority of which has no faith, is entirely positivist in outlook, but even the positivists fail to notice the absurdity of the Marxist thesis that the Universe exists for ever while the Earth is merely fortuitous. Contemporary man is unable to hope for the unexpected, for anomalous events that don't correspond with 'normal' logic; still less is he prepared to allow even the thought of unprogrammed phenomena, let alone believe in their supernatural significance. The spiritual emptiness that results should be enough to give him pause for thought. First, however, he has to understand that his life's path is not measured by a human yardstick but lies in the hands of the Creator, on whose will he must rely.

One of the greatest tragedies of the modern world is the fact that moral problems and ethical interrelationships are not in fashion; they have receded into the background and command little attention. A great many producers eschew *auteur* films because they see cinema not as art but as a means of making money; the celluloid strip becomes a commodity. [p. 228]

Not even the Church can quench man's thirst for the Absolute, for unfortunately it only exists as a kind of appendage, copying or even caricaturing the social institutions by which our everyday life is organized. Certainly in today's world which leans so heavily towards the material and the technological, the Church shows no sign of being able to redress the balance with a call to a spiritual awakening. [p. 237]

Certainly each successive catastrophe is evidence that the civilization in question was misconceived; and when man is forced to start all over again, it can only be because up till then he has had as his aim something other than spiritual perfection.

In a sense art is an image of the completed process, of the culmination; an imitation of the possession of absolute truth (albeit only in the form of an image) obviating the long – perhaps, indeed, endless – path of history.

There are moments when one longs to rest, to hand it all over, to give it up, along with oneself, to some total world-view – like the Veda, for instance. The East was closer to the truth than the West; but Western civilization devoured the East with its materialist demands on life.

Compare Eastern and Western music. The West is forever shouting, 'This is me! Look at me! Listen to me suffering, loving! How unhappy I am! How Happy! I! Mine! Me!' In the Eastern tradition they never utter a word about themselves. The person is totally absorbed into God, Nature, Time; finding himself in everything; discovering everything in himself. Think of Taoist music...China six hundred years before Christ...But in that case, why did such a superb idea not triumph, why did it collapse? Why did the civilization that grew up on such a foundation not come down to us in the form of a historic process brought to its consummation? They must have come into conflict with the materialistic world that surrounded them. Just as the personality comes into conflict with society, that civilization clashed with another. It perished not only for that reason, but also because of its confrontation with the materialist world of 'progress' and technology. But the civilization was the final point of true knowledge, salt of the salt of the earth. And according to the logic of Eastern thought, conflict of any kind is essentially sinful. [pp. 240–41]

THE CINEMATIC POEM – A SHORT FILM PROJECT

I have still not given up hope of a short film one day: I even have some rough drafts in my note-book. One of these is a poem by my father, Arseny Alexandrovich Tarkovsky, which he himself was to have read. Although now, of course, I don't even know if I shall ever see him again. In the meantime I have used it in *Nostalgia*:

As a child I once fell ill
With hunger and fear. Off my lips I peeled
Hard scales, and licked my lips. I remember
Still the taste of it, saltish and cool.
And all the time I walked and walked and walked,
Sat down on the front stairs to warm myself,
Walked my lightheaded way as if dancing
To the rat-catcher's tune, riverwards. Sat down
To warm on the stairs, shivering every which way.
And mother stands there beckoning, looks as if
She's close, but I can't go up to her:
I move towards her, she stands seven steps away,
Beckons me; I move towards her, she stands
Seven steps away and beckons me.
I felt too hot,
Undid my collar button and lay down,
Then there were trumpets blaring, light beating
Down on my eyelids, horses galloping, mother
Was flying above the roadway, beckoned me
And flew away...
And now my dream is of
A hospital, white beneath the apple trees,
And a white sheet beneath my chin,
And a white doctor looking down at me,
And a white nurse standing at my feet
And her wings moving. And there they stayed.
And mother came, and beckoned me –
And flew away...

Long ago I thought of using the following sequence for the poem.

Scene 1: Establishing shot. Aerial view of a town; autumn or early winter. Slow zoom in to a tree standing by the stucco wall of a monastery.

Scene 2: Close shot. Low angle shot, zoom in to puddles, grass, moss, shot in close-up to give the effect of a landscape. In the first shot town noises can be heard – harsh and insistent – these die away completely by the end of the 2nd shot.

Scene 3: Close shot. A bonfire. Someone's hand stretches out an old, crumpled envelope towards the dying flame. The fire flares up. The camera tilts for a low angle shot of the father (the author of the poem), standing by a tree and looking at the fire. Then he bends down, evidently to tend the fire. The shot widens to a broad, autumnal landscape. The sky is overcast. Far away the bonfire is burning in the middle of the field. The father is poking it. He straightens up, turns, and walks away from the camera over the fields. Slow zoom from behind to medium shot. The father walks on. All the time the zoom lens shows him the same size. Then he gradually turns until he is shown in profile. The father vanishes into the trees. From out of the trees, and continuing along the father's path, appears the son. Gradual zoom in to the son's face, which by the end of the shot is just in front of the camera.

Scene 4: From the point of view of the son. Elevation shot and zoom in: roads, puddles, withered grass. A white feather falls, circling, down into a puddle.
(I used the feather in *Nostalgia*.)

Scene 5: Close-up. The son looks at the fallen feather, and then up at the sky. He bends, then straightens up and walks out of frame. Pull focus to long shot: the son picks up the feather and walks on. He vanishes into the trees, from which, walking in the same direction, appears the poet's grandson. In his hand is a white feather. Dusk is falling. The grandson walks over the field. Zoom in to close-up of the grandson, in profile; he suddenly notices something out of frame and stops. Pan in the direction of his gaze. Long shot of an angel standing at the edge of the darkening forest. Dusk is falling. Darkness descends as the focus blurs.

The poem can be heard from about the beginning of the third shot up to the end of the fourth; between the bonfire and the falling feather. Almost at the moment when the poem finishes, perhaps a little earlier, can be heard the end of the finale of Haydn's 'Farewell Symphony', which comes to an end as darkness falls. [pp. 91–93]

Source: Andrey Tarkovsky, *Sculpting in Time: Reflections on the Cinema*, translated by Kitty Hunter-Blair, London, 1986.

The Films

COMMENTARIES BY HANS-JOACHIM SCHLEGEL

ABBREVIATIONS:

S = Screenplay | SA = Script assistant | C = Cinematographer | CA = Camera assistant | Ed = Editor | So = Sound | SM = Sound mixer | M = Music | PD = Production design | SD = Set design | CD = Costume design | Ma = Make-up | AD = Assistant director | DA = Director's assistant | PC = Production company | P = Producer | Co-P = Co-producer | PM = Production manager | PS = Production supervisor | Loc = Location | F = Format | b&w = black and white | RT = Running time

Ivan's Childhood

IVANOVO DETSTVO 1962

Cinematography: Vadim Iusov

S: Vladimir Bogomolov, Mikhail Papava, based on the short story 'Ivan' by Vladimir Bogomolov | SA: E. Smirnov | C: Vadim Iusov | Ed: Lyudmila Feiginova | So: E. Zelentsova | M: Vyacheslav Ovchinnikov | Conductor: Emin Khachaturian | PD: Yevgeni Chernyaev | Ma: L. Baskakova | AD: Georgi Natanson | Special effects: V. Sevostyanov, S. Mukhin | Military advisor: G. Goncharov | Script ed: E. Smirnov

Cast: Nikolai (Kolya) Burlyaev (Ivan), Valentin Zubkov (Kholin), Y. Zharikov (Galtsev), S. Krylov (Katasonov), Nikolai Grinko (Gryaznov), V. Maliavina (Masha), Irma Raush Tarkovskaya (Ivan's Mother), D. Miliutenko (Old Man), Andrei Mikhalkov Konchalovsky (Soldier), Ivan Savkin, V. Marenkov, Vera Miturich | PC: Mosfilm | PM: G. Kuznetsov | Filmed: 15 June 1961–18 January 1962 | F: 35 mm, b&w | RT: 97 min | Premiere: 6 April 1962, Moscow

First screening outside the USSR: October 1962, Venice Film Festival (winner of the Golden Lion)

Tarkovsky took over an unfinished Mosfilm studio project that had originally been directed by Eduard Abalov, and wrote a new screenplay in collaboration with Vladimir Bogomolov, author of the original short story.

On the Ukrainian front, some Russian soldiers find a twelve-year-old boy who has just returned from doing reconnaissance behind German lines. Through flashbacks and dream sequences we learn that his father was killed at the beginning of the war, his mother and sister probably died as a result of a German retaliatory strike, and he himself escaped from a death camp. Traumatized and driven by a desire for revenge, Ivan shuts himself off from the frontline officer who has taken a fatherly interest in him, and refuses to go to a military school in the hinterland. During a night-time patrol through swampy country along the Dnieper river, Ivan insists on cutting down the bodies of soldiers who have been hanged by the Germans, and then disappears in the mist and rain, heading for the German front. A sequence of sharply cut documentary scenes shows the triumphant Soviet conquest of Berlin, the occupation of the Reichstag, and the bodies of Goebbels' children. Soviet soldiers discover files containing photographs of people the Gestapo have murdered – and these include Ivan.

Kolya Burlyaev
Ivan

Valentin Zubkov
Kholin

Irma Raush Tarkovskaya
Ivan's Mother

Добро

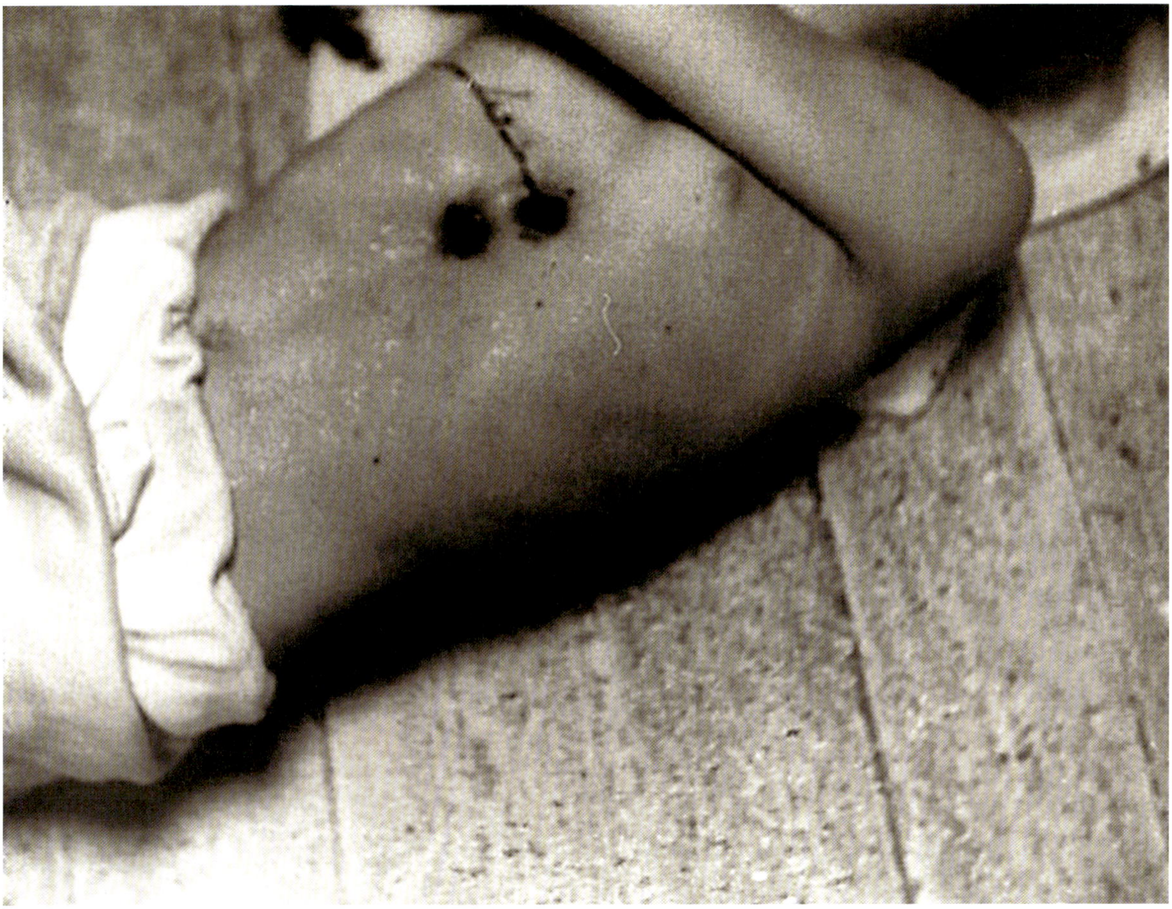

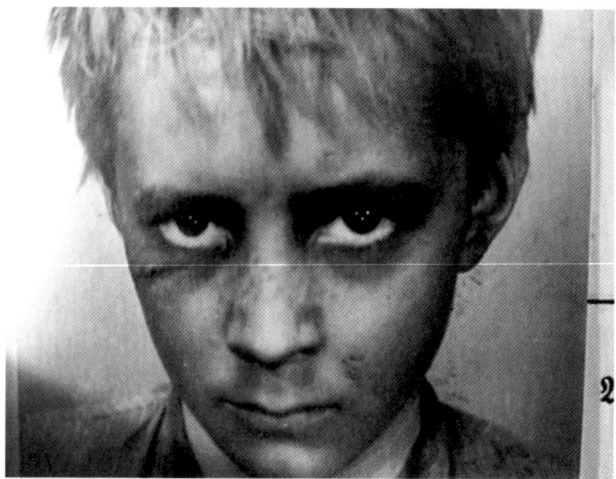

Andrei Rublev

ANDREY RUBLYOV 1964–66

Cinematography: Vadim Iusov

S: Andrei Mikhalkov Konchalovsky, Andrey Tarkovsky | C: Vadim Iusov | Ed: Lyudmila Feiginova, T. Yegorychova, O. Shevkunenko | So: E. Zelentsova | M: Vyacheslav Ovchinnikov | PD: Yevgeni Chernyaev, with I. Novoderezhkin, S. Voronkov | CD: L. Novi, M. Abar-Baranovskaia | AD: I. Petrov | DA: Bagrat Oganesyan, A. Macharet, M. Volovich | Camera operator: V. Sevostyanov

Cast: Anatoli Solonitsyn (Andrei Rublev), Ivan Lapikov (Kirill), Nikolai Grinko (Daniel the Black), Nikolai Sergeyev (Theophanes the Greek), Irma Raush Tarkovskaya (Idiot girl/holy fool), Nikolai (Kolya) Burlyaev (Boriska), Yuri Nazarov (Grand Duke/Lesser Duke), Rolan Bykov (Jester), Bolot Beyshenaliyev (Tatar Khan), Yuri Nikulin (Patrikey), Mikhail Kononov (Fomka), Stepan Krylov (Bell-founder), Sos Sarkisyan (Christ), N. Grabbe, B. Matisik, A. Obukhov, V. Titov, N. Glazkov, K. Aleksandrov, S. Bardin, I. Bykov, G. Borisovsky, V. Vasilyev, Z. Vorkul, V. Volkov, A. Titov, I. Miroshnichenko, T. Ogorodnikova

PC: Mosfilm | P: T. Ogorodnikova | Filmed: 9 September 1964–November 1966 | F: 35 mm, b&w and colour (Sovcolor) | RT: 185 min; 1st part: 86 min; 2nd part: 99 min | Premiere: late 1966, Moscow | Cinema screening: 17 February 1969, Dom Cinema, Moscow; Full release: 19 October 1971 | First screening outside the USSR: May 1969, Cannes Film Festival (out of competition)

Tarkovsky cut several different versions of the film. The first cut was 5,624 m long, the second cut 5,250 m, and the third cut, which was identical to the version shown at Cannes, 5,076 m long (185 min). Aside from a single 1969 screening in a Moscow cinema, the film was not released in the USSR until 1971 and was not distributed internationally until 1973. Friedrich Gorenstein (uncredited in the film) wrote the scene in which Andrei Rublev meets Theophanes the Greek. Under Soviet protest, the film was shown at the Cannes Film Festival in 1969 where it won the FIPRESCI prize from international film critics.

A prologue in which a farmer named Jefim falls to his death as he attempts to fly a homemade hot-air balloon is followed by eight chapters from the life of the Russian monk and icon painter Andrei Rublev between 1400 and 1423.

The Jester, 1400: In search of work as icon painters, the monks Andrei Rublev, Kirill and Daniel the Black witness soldiers of the Grand Duke abducting an entertainer who has mocked His Highness, and smashing his musical instruments.

Theophanes the Greek, 1405–6: The entertainer is executed in a village square. The old icon painter Theophanes the Greek offers Kirill a job as an assistant on the painting of the Cathedral of the Annunciation in Moscow. Kirill asks Theophanes to give him the post in the presence of Andrei Rublev, and is then very bitter when it is Andrei who is chosen for the job. He storms out of the monastery, cursing the clergy.

The Passion According to Andrei, 1406: On their way to Moscow, Theophanes, Andrei Rublev and the latter's pupil Fomka discuss theological issues. Unlike Theophanes, who wishes to turn his back on the vanities of earthly life and artistic endeavour, and 'to serve God alone', Rublev's desire is to serve his fellow men and relieve hunger, disease and the sufferings inflicted by the Tatars.

The Feast, 1408: At night Rublev and his assistants find themselves involved in a pantheistic orgy in celebration of spring. As a supposed agent of the Church, Rublev is tied to a cross. Marfa, a young woman who has fallen in love with him, releases him, rejects his attempts to convert her, and at daybreak is killed during a brutal assault by the soldiers of the Grand Duke.

The Last Judgment, 1408: The Grand Duke goes to see the frescoes that are being painted in the cathedral in Vladimir, where the artists are quarrelling about their

Anatoli Solonitsyn
Andrei Rublev

Ivan Lapikov
Kirill

Nikolai Grinko
Daniel the Black

Irma Raush Tarkovskaya
Idiot girl ('holy fool')

Rolan Bykov
Jester

Stepan Krylov
Bell-founder

work. Rublev does not want to add to the sufferings of the people with images of hell's torments. Soldiers put out the eyes of the migrant painters so they will not be able to work for the Grand Duke's younger brother.

The Raid, 1408: The Grand Duke's younger brother, in a bid to gain the title for himself, enters a treacherous alliance with the Tatars, and with their help conquers Vladimir, where those people who have sought refuge in the cathedral are brutally massacred. The Tatars torture the sexton to death because he refuses to reveal the location of the treasury. When a Russian soldier attempts to rape a mentally ill girl (a 'holy fool'), Andrei Rublev kills him, and because he has committed a mortal sin he takes a vow of silence and swears to the spirit of the now deceased Theophanes that he will never paint again.

The Silence, 1412: In a Russia that has been laid waste by starvation and the Tatars, the exhausted and contrite Kirill returns to the monastery. Meanwhile, Rublev maintains his vow of silence. The Tatars are celebrating in the courtyard of the monastery, and when they leave they take with them the 'holy fool', who has followed Rublev after he had rescued her.

The Bell, 1423–24: To mark the new peace, the Grand Duke decides to have a colossal bell cast. He can find no one to do the job except a young boy, who claims to have learned the art from his father. Full of admiration, Rublev watches the meticulous and passionate way the boy sets about his work. When at last the great bell is consecrated before the Grand Duke and various foreign envoys, it rings with a sound of astonishing beauty. Rublev ends his vow of silence, decides to paint icons again and to work with the boy, who is to make more bells.

The film ends with the camera panning slowly over Rublev's icons and frescoes and a rainswept river landscape with grazing horses.

Solaris

SOLYARIS 1971–72

Cinematography: Vadim Iusov

S: Friedrich Gorenstein, Andrey Tarkovsky, based on the novel *Solaris* by Stanislaw Lem | C: Vadim Iusov | Camera operator: E. Shvedov | Ed: Lyudmila Feiginova | So: Semyon Litvinov | M: Eduard Artemiev (variation on the *Prelude in F Minor* by Johann Sebastian Bach) | SD: Mikhail Romadin | CD: N. Fomina | Ma: V. Rudina | 2nd Director: Y. Kushneryov | DA: A. Ides, Larisa Tarkovskaya, M. Chugunova | Special effects: A. Klimenko, V. Sevostyanov

Cast: Natalya Bondarchuk (Hari), Donatas Banionis (Kris Kelvin), Yuri Järvet (Snauth), Anatoli Solonitsyn (Sartorius), Nikolai Grinko (Kelvin's Father), Sos Sarkisyan (Gibarian), Vladislav Dvorzhetsky (Berton), O. Barnet, V. Kerdimun, T. Ogorodnikova, O. Kizilova, T. Malykh, A. Misharin, B. Oganesyan, Y. Semyonov, V. Statsinsky, S. Sumenova, G. Teykh

PC: Mosfilm | P: Viacheslav Tarasov | Filmed: May 1971 | Loc: Mosfilm Studio/Pavilion 5; Zvenigorod district; Crimean coast; Ruza river | F: 35 mm, b&w and colour (Sovcolor) | RT: 167 min | Premiere: 5 February 1973, Moscow | First screening outside the USSR: May 1972, Cannes Film Festival (Grand Prix du Jury)

The film is based on themes drawn from Stanislaw Lem's science-fiction novel of the same name. The psychologist Kris Kelvin is sent to evaluate the state of mind of the astrobiologist Sartorius, the cybernetician Snauth and the physiologist Gibarian on a space station orbiting the planet Solaris. Before he sets off, he goes to his father's lake house, where he meets the Solaris expert Henri Berton, who is thought to be crazy because he insists that above the planet's 'ocean' he has seen a garden and a child four metres tall. The two men have an inconclusive argument about the moral responsibility of science.

On the dilapidated space station, Snauth – who is now a nervous wreck – tells Kelvin that Gibarian has committed suicide, but has left behind a video about his plans to make contact with the 'ocean'. Strange 'beings' turn up at Sartorius's cabin, and eventually Hari – who resembles a girl in a video of his childhood Kelvin has brought with him – appears too. She loves Kelvin, and during Snauth's birthday party she takes his side against Sartorius's cold, rational cynicism. In a feverish dream, Kelvin sees himself as a child with his young mother. Meanwhile, Hari has allowed herself to be 'annihilated' by Sartorius, and the other 'beings' have also disappeared. It seems that with the encephalogram of his conscious and unconscious thoughts Kelvin has been able to calm the plasma of the 'ocean'. He talks with Snauth about happiness, death and love, and finally is back in the garden of the lake house, where he kneels and embraces his father. A long shot then reveals that the house and garden are an island in the cosmic Solaris ocean.

Donatas Banionis
Kris Kelvin

Vladislav Dvorzhetsky
Berton

Sos Sarkisyan
Gibarian

Natalya Bondarchuk
Hari

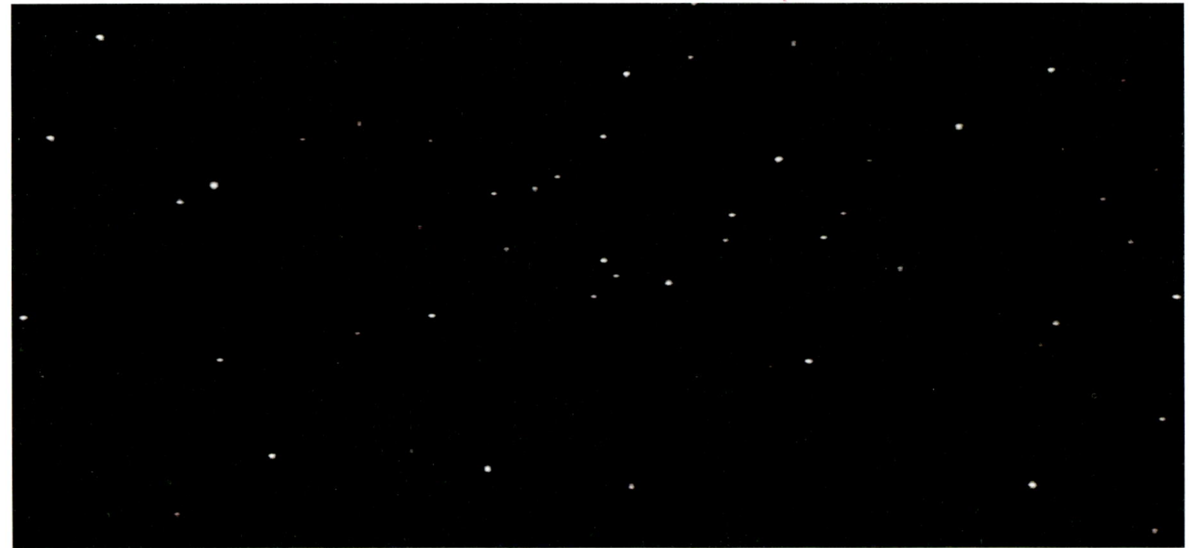

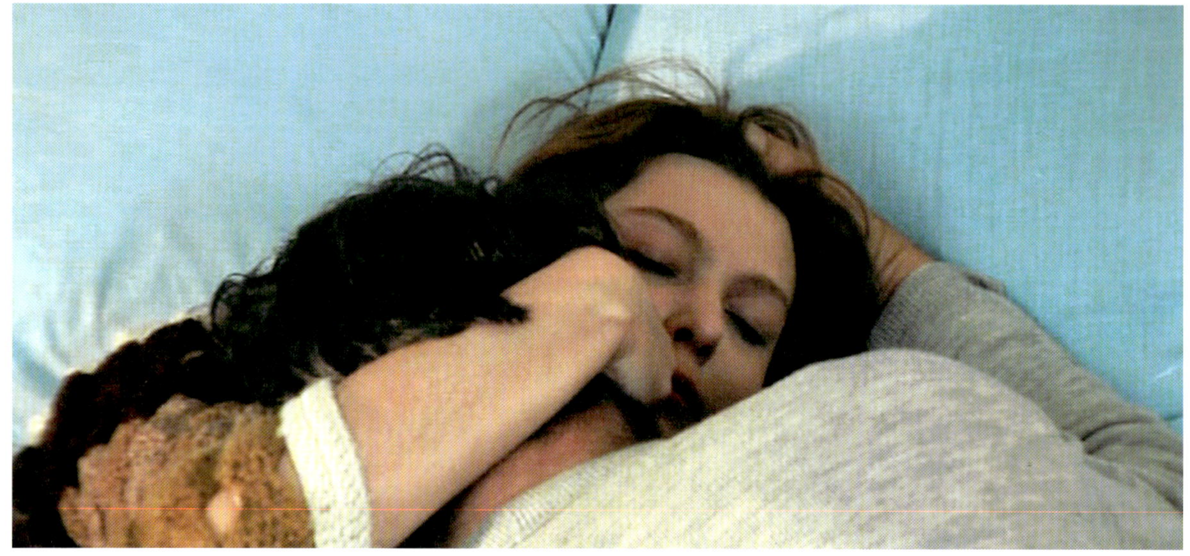

Mirror

ZERKALO 1973–74

Cinematography: Georgi Rerberg

S: Aleksandr Misharin, Andrey Tarkovsky | C: Georgi Rerberg | 2nd Camera: A. Nikolaev, I. Shtanko | Ed: Lyudmila Feiginova | T: Semyon Litvinov | M: Eduard Artemiev, Johann Sebastian Bach, Henry Purcell, Giovanni Battista Pergolesi | PD: Nikolai Dvigubsky | SD: A. Merkulov | CD: N. Fomina | Ma: V. Rudina | AD: Y. Kushneryov | DA: Larisa Tarkovskaya, V. Kharchenko, M. Chugunova | Special effects: Yuri Potapov

The film includes extracts from documentary footage by Soviet cameramen of the Red Army marching across the Sivash marshes in 1943; from Roman Karmen and Esther Shub's documentary footage of the Spanish Civil War; and from newsreels covering the arrival of the Red Army in Prague and Berlin in 1945, the Soviet-Chinese conflict in Ussuri and the Cultural Revolution in Mao Zedong's China.

Cast: Margarita Terekhova (Mother/Natalya), Ignat Daniltsev (Alexei, the narrator as a child/Ignat, the narrator's son), Oleg Yankovsky (Narrator's Father), Filip Yankovsky (Alexei, aged 5), Alla Demidova (Lisa), Anatoli Solonitsyn (Forensic Doctor), Nikolai Grinko (Printing House Director), Tamara Ogorodnikova (Neighbour), Yuri Nazarov (Military Trainer), Larisa Tarkovskaya, Yuri Sventikov, T. Reshetnikova, E. del Bosque, L. Correcher, A. Gutiérrez, D. Garcia, T. Pames, Teresa del Bosque, Tatiana del Bosque, Innokenti Smoktunovsky (Narrato r's voice), Maria Ivanovna Vishnyakova Tarkovskaya as herself, Arseny Tarkovsky reading his own poems.

PC: Mosfilm | P: Erik Waisberg | Filmed: September 1973–March 1974 | F: 35 mm, b&w and colour (Sovcolor) | RT: 108 min | Premiere: April 1975, Moscow

---

This distinctly autobiographical film, with its associative structure, begins with a prologue in which a speech therapist cures a stammer by hypnosis; the scene ends with a statement of liberation: 'I can speak.'

In the first scene, a young woman named Maria, who is the mother of the narrator Alexei, is looking across the fields; a doctor arrives and talks to her about the spirit of nature. Next she is sitting with Alexei in the farmhouse as a barn burns in the pouring rain outside. Alexei calls out: 'Papa!' The mother washes her hair, the ceiling caves in, and the rain comes into the room.

In the next scene, the mother tells Alexei over the phone that his father left her in the year when the barn burned down, and now a colleague at the printing firm where she worked as a proofreader has died. A poster of Stalin conjures up the terror of the period. Alexei quarrels with his wife Natalya, whose face resembles that of his mother in his dreams of his childhood. Refugees from the Spanish Civil War arrive in the flat; this is followed by documentary footage of a bullfight and the evacuation of Spanish children from the bombed ruins of Madrid.

A woman asks Ignat, Alexei and Natalya's son, to read out a letter written by Pushkin about Russia's role as the defender of European Christianity against Asia.

Next we see the teenage Alexei and a red-haired girl with a harelip at shooting practice. A boy who lost his parents in the siege of Leningrad throws a dummy hand grenade. There is documentary footage of Soviet soldiers wading through the shallow Lake Sivash, a celebratory firework display outside the Berlin Reichstag, the atom bomb being dropped on Bikini Atoll, Maoists marching in Beijing, and the Russian-Chinese border clashes on the banks of the Ussuri river. Inserted amid all these is a scene based on Bruegel's *Winter Landscape*. Alexei's father comes home on leave from the front and embraces his children.

Alexei and Natalya are now separated, and quarrel over who is to have custody of their son Ignat. Out in the yard, Ignat lights a fire in the rain.

Margarita Terekhova
Mother/Natalya

Ignat Daniltsev
*Alexei, the narrator as a child/
Ignat, the narrator's son*

Filip Yankovsky
Alexei, aged 5

Maria Ivanovna Vishnyakova Tarkovskaya
Tarkovsky's mother as herself

Alexei dreams of his childhood on his grandfather's farm, where he and his mother were evacuated during the war. His mother tries to persuade the pregnant wife of a doctor to accept her earrings in exchange for some food. Lost in thought, Alexei – who has been left on his own – gazes at some spilled milk, his reflection, and a fire. His mother has to chop the head off a chicken. She dreams that her husband is caressing her. She hovers above the marriage bed. Then quickly she leaves the house with Alexei.

ANDREI ROUBL
LE FILM DE

Stalker

STALKER 1978–79

Cinematography: Aleksandr Knyazhinsky

S: Arkady Strugatsky, Boris Strugatsky, based on the novella *Piknik na obotschine* (*Roadside Picnic*) | C: Aleksandr Knyazhinsky | Camera operator: N. Fudim, S. Naugolnykh | CA: G. Verkhovsky, S. Zaitsev | Ed: Lyudmila Feiginova | So: V. Sharun | M: Eduard Artemiev, *Bolero* by Maurice Ravel, *Symphony No. 9* by Ludwig van Beethoven | Conductor: E. Khachaturian | Main PD: Andrey Tarkovsky | PD: R. Safiullin, V. Fabrikov | SD: A. Merkulov | CD: N. Fomina | Ma: V. Luova | AD: Larisa Tarkovskaya | DA: M. Chugunova, E. Tsimbal

Cast: Aleksandr Kaidanovsky (Stalker), Anatoli Solonitsyn (Writer), Nikolai Grinko (Professor), Alisa Freindlikh (Stalker's Wife), Natasha Abramova (Martha, Stalker's Daughter), F. Yurna, E. Kostin, R. Rendi

PC: Mosfilm | P: Aleksandra Demidova | Loc: Near Tallinn, Estonia, and near Isfara, Tajikistan | F: 35 mm, colour (Sovcolor) | RT: 163 min | Premiere: August 1979, Moscow Film Festival | First screening outside the USSR: 13 May 1980, Cannes Film Festival

In a mysterious place called the Zone, virtually inaccessible from the outside world, there is said to be a room where all wishes are fulfilled. Stalker, the only person who knows the rules and dangers of this extraterrestrial region, is to take a writer and a professor to it. The route leads past fragments and remnants of a ruined civilization. The professor and writer discuss the limitations of technology and rationality and Stalker talks about music, while off screen we hear a poem written by Tarkovsky's father Arseny. In the antechamber leading to the wishing room, the trio quarrel about the room's meaning and function. The professor sees it as a place of imminent human catastrophe and wants to destroy it, but he allows Stalker to talk him out of it. The three men find themselves back at the starting point of their expedition. Tired and ill, Stalker complains about the human scepticism that makes his mission pointless, whereas his wife believes that the meaning of their miserable life lies in hope. Their handicapped daughter is able to move glasses using the telekinetic power of her eyes. The sounds of a train mingle with the 'Ode to Joy' from Beethoven's *Symphony No. 9*.

Aleksandr Kaidanovsky
Stalker

Anatoli Solonitsyn
Writer

Nikolai Grinko
Professor

Natasha Abramova
Martha, Stalker's Daughter

Alisa Freindlikh
Stalker's Wife

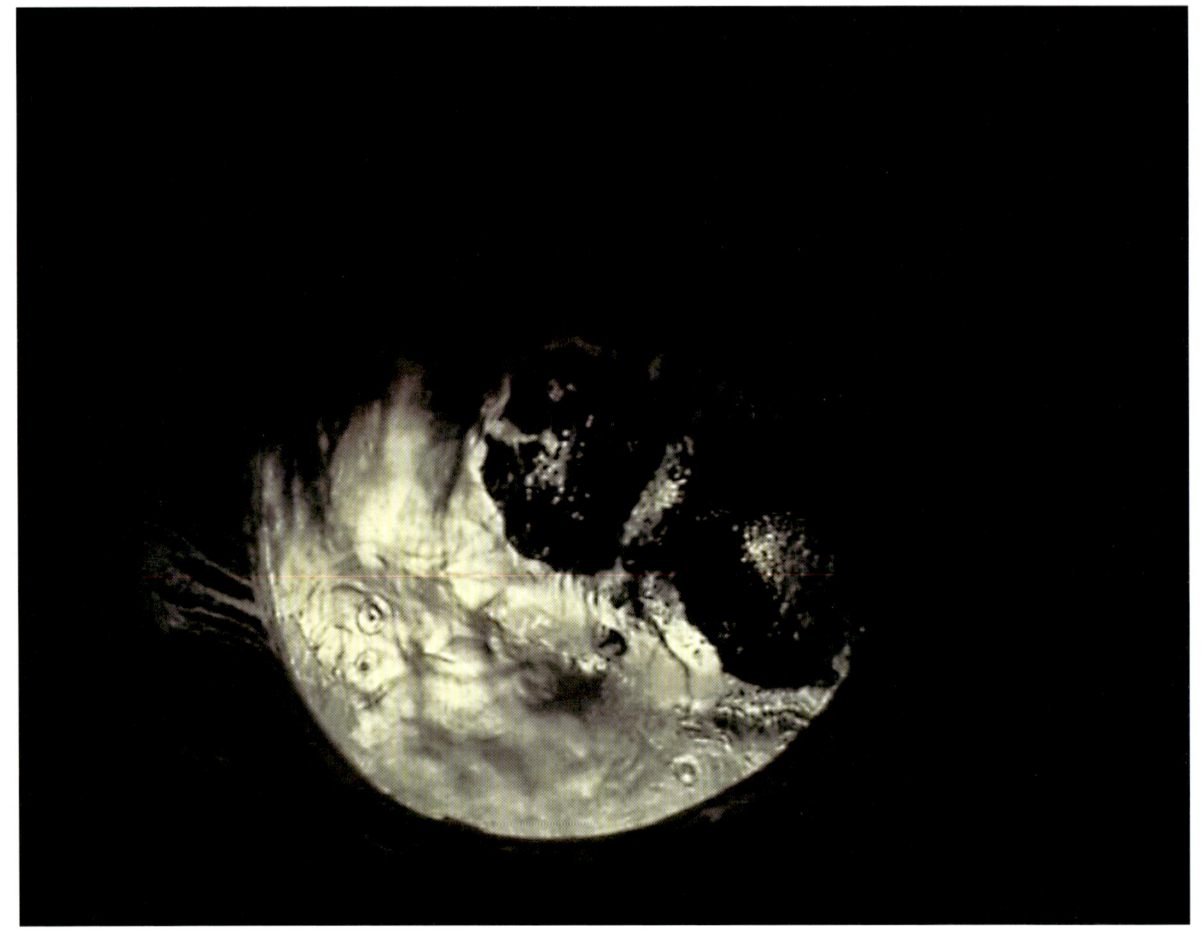

Nostalgia

NOSTALGHIA 1982–83

Cinematography: Giuseppe Lanci

S: Andrey Tarkovsky, Tonino Guerra | C: Giuseppe Lanci | Camera operator: Giuseppe de Biase | CA: Giancarlo Battaglia, Luigi Cecchini | Ed: Amedeo Salfa, Erminia Marani | S: Remo Ugolinelli | SM: Fausto Ancillai | Sound effects: Luciano Anzellotti, Massimo Anzellotti | M: Claude Debussy, Giuseppe Verdi, Richard Wagner, Ludwig van Beethoven | Music consultant: Gino Peguri | PD: Andrea Crisanti | SD: Mauro Passi | CD: Lina Nerli Taviani | Ma: Giulio Mastrantonio | DA: Norman Mozzato, Larisa Tarkovskaya | Special effects: Paolo Ricci

Cast: Oleg Yankovsky (Andrei Gorchakov), Domiziana Giordano (Eugenia), Erland Josephson (Domenico), Patrizia Terreno (Andrei's Wife), Laura De Marchi (Chambermaid), Delia Boccardo (Domenico's Wife), Milena Vukotic (Civil Servant), Alberto Canepa (Peasant)

PC: RAI, Rete2/Opera Film, Rome | P: Francesco Casati | PS: Filippo Campus, Valentino Signoretti | Filmed: November 1982–May 1983 | Loc: Bagno Vignoni, Rome | F: 35 mm, colour (Technicolor), b&w | RT: 130 min | Premiere: May 1983, Cannes Film Festival (winner of Special Jury Prize, Prize for Best Direction, and FIPRESCI Prize)

In present-day Italy, the Russian writer Andrei Gorchakov is looking for information about the life of the composer Pavel Sosnovsky, whose patron had sent him there during the 19th century. However, he himself falls victim to the melancholy of loneliness and homesickness. He meets Domenico, a former maths teacher, who is regarded as mad because he had shut himself and his family up at home to escape from the end of the world. After a tirade against the lunacy of modern civilization, Domenico sets himself on fire in front of the Roman statue of Marcus Aurelius. Gorchakov sets out to fulfil Domenico's wish that he should carry a burning candle across a dried-up thermal spring. When he finally reaches the other side, he falls down dead.

Domiziana Giordano
Eugenia

Oleg Yankovsky
Andrei Gorchakov

Erland Josephson
Domenico

The Sacrifice

OFFRET 1985–86

Cinematography: Sven Nykvist

S: Andrey Tarkovsky | C: Sven Nykvist | CA: Lars Karlsson, Dan Myhrman | Ed: Andrey Tarkovsky, Michal Leszczylowski | So, SM: Owe Svensson, Bo Persson | M: Johann Sebastian Bach: Aria 'Erbarme Dich' from the *St Matthew Passion* (Alto: Julia Hamari; Conductor: Wolfgang Gönnenwein); Japanese instrumental music (Hotchiku flute: Watazumido Shuso); Swedish folk music (vocalists: Elin Lisslass, Karin Edvards Johansson, Tjugmyr Maria Larsson) | SD: Anna Asp | CD: Inger Pehrsson | Ma: Kjell Gustavsson, Florence Fouquier | DA: Kerstin Eriksdotter | Special effects: Svenska Stuntgruppen, Lars Hoglund, Lars Palmqvist

Cast: Erland Josephson (Alexander), Susan Fleetwood (Adelaide), Valérie Mairesse (Julia), Allan Edwall (Otto), Gudrún Gísladóttir (Maria), Sven Wollter (Victor), Filippa Franzén (Marta), Tommy Kjellqvist (Boy)

PC: Svenska Filminstitutet, Stockholm/Argos Films, Paris | Co-P: Film Four International, London/Josephson & Nykvist HB, Stockholm, Sveriges Telev. SVT 2, Stockholm/Sandrew Film & Theater AB, Stockholm; with the support of the French Ministry of Culture | P: Anna-Lena Wisbom (Svenska Filminstitutet) | PM: Katinka Faragó (Faragó Film AB) | Filmed: May–July 1985 | Loc: island of Gotland (exteriors), Studio Filmhuset, Stockholm (interiors) | F: 35 mm, colour (Eastmancolor) | RT: 145 min | Premiere: 9 May 1986, Stockholm | 1986 Cannes Film Festival, winner of the FIPRESCI Prize, the Grand Prix du Jury, the Prize of the Ecumenical Jury and an award for Best Artistic Contribution for cinematographer Sven Nykvist.

Alexander has given up his career in the theatre and the classroom, and he and his English wife Adelaide have withdrawn from the world to live in a wooden house on a remote island. Adelaide is not happy about it. On his birthday, Alexander welcomes some guests and with his six-year-old son plants a withered tree, which according to an old monastic legend is supposed to blossom again if it is watered regularly, accompanied by a holy ritual. Suddenly the sky darkens and the TV news announces a global catastrophe. Alexander vows to God that he will leave his family, destroy his house and never speak again if 'everything returns to what it was before, this morning, yesterday.' He sleeps with a 'white witch' and wakes up in the morning in a world which is as it was before. He keeps his promise, burns the house down, and allows himself to be taken away by medical attendants.

His son, who has been mute ever since he had an operation on his larynx, lies under the withered tree and is able to speak again: 'In the beginning was the Word. Why, Papa?'

Erland Josephson
Alexander

Susan Fleetwood
Adelaide

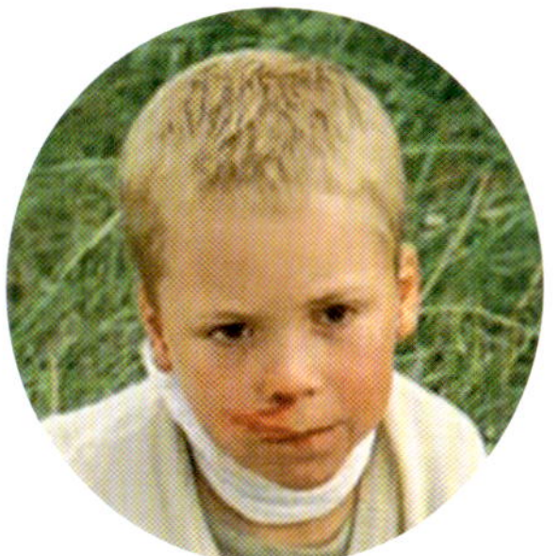

Tommy Kjellqvist
Boy

Gudrún Gísladóttir
Maria

Valérie Mairesse
Julia

JVC
JVC

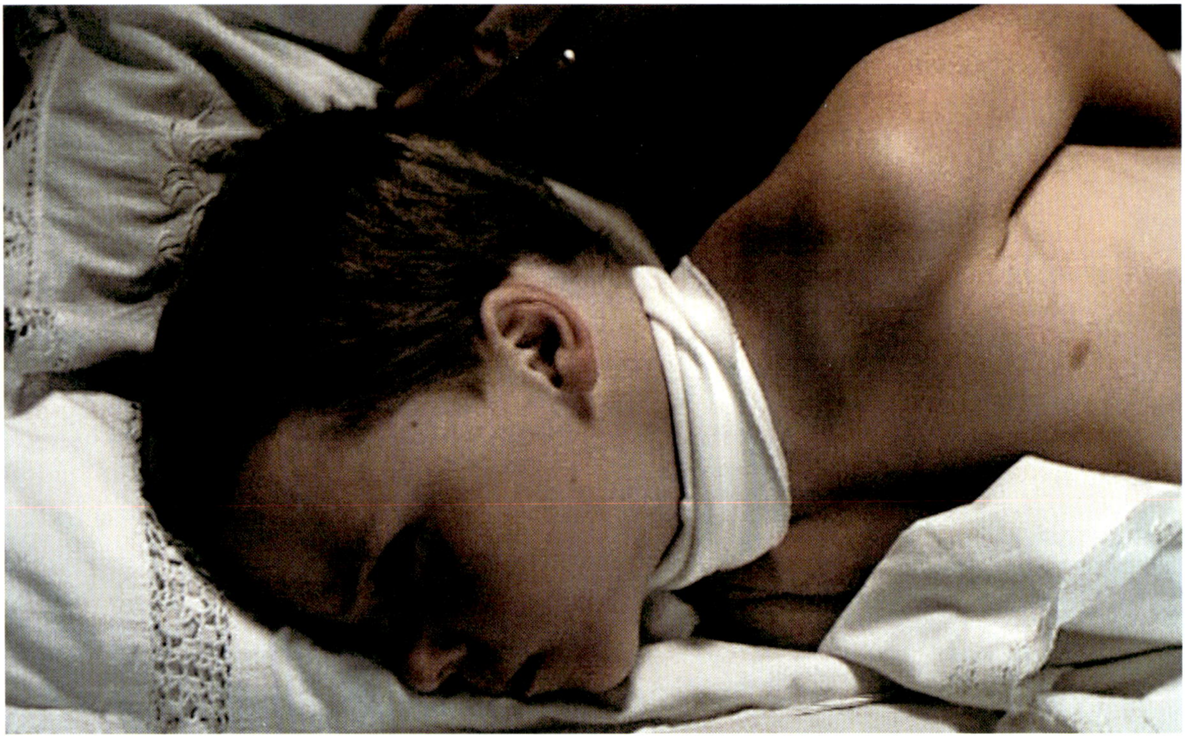

JVC
JVC

Autobiographical Writings

ANDREY TARKOVSKY

RÉSUMÉ

I was born on 4 April 1932 by the River Volga, in the town of Yurevets, Ivanovo Region. My father, Arseny Aleksandrovich Tarkovsky, is a poet and translator and a member of the Union of Soviet Writers. He is a decorated World War II veteran and invalid. My mother, Maria Ivanovna Vishnyakova, now works as a proofreader at Zhdanov Printing Press.

In 1939 I started at school No. 554 in Moskvoretsky District, Moscow. During the war my mother took my sister and myself back to the place where I was born on the Volga (we were evacuated). There, in Yurevets, I attended primary school No. 1. In 1949 we returned to Moscow and I re-entered school No. 554. While at school I studied music (from the age of seven). When I was in my seventh year there, I also studied painting for a time.

I studied music at the district music school in Leninsky District, Moscow, and painting at the 1905 Memorial Art School.

I took part in school drama productions (and later in student ones). I played the part of Netsvetaev in Barianov's play *On the Other Side*, Count Lampetri in Petrov's play *Mister Volk*, Levko in *May Night*, and other lesser roles. After leaving school in 1951 I enrolled at the Institute of Oriental Studies, where I studied for eighteen months. However, in 1952, due to concussion suffered during a PE lesson, I fell behind with my studies and had to abandon the course.

However, when I was at the institute I often thought that my choice of profession had been rather hasty. I did not yet know enough about life.

I became really interested in cinema and literature, but most of all in our country's people, its natural environment and its way of life. I therefore decided against going back to the Institute of Oriental Studies, and in May 1953 got a job with a scientific expedition from the NIGRIzoloto Institute, going off to work in eastern Siberia. I stayed with the expedition for a year in the Turukhansk Taiga, travelling hundreds of kilometres. That expedition provided many interesting experiences. I met many people, both geologists and ordinary workers. There I learned the difficult but noble work of geologists, geomorphologists and geophysicists. All this strengthened my resolve to become a film director. In April 1954 I finished my work with the expedition. As well as collecting, I kept a sketchbook of Siberian landscapes, which is now in the NIGRIzoloto Institute archives. My work concluded with the processing of field materials in Moscow (attached is a reference from the group's chief geologist). I then started preparing for the VGIK entrance exams. In spring 1954, in an attempt to find out more about the VGIK course, I took part in filming at the institute's teaching studio (the role of team captain in the section about basketball players). I now dream of becoming a good director of Soviet cinema.

Written when applying for the VGIK film school, 23 July 1954. Source: M. Rostotskaia (ed.), *Andrey Tarkovsky. Beginnings...and Journey*, VGIK, Moscow, 1994, pp. 10–11.

ON HIS MOTHER

Father had a certain inner influence on me, but of course I owe everything to my mother. It was she who helped me to fulfil myself. In the film [*Mirror*], one can see that we lived a difficult life in what was generally a difficult time. When mother was left on her own, I was three years old and my sister was one and a half. She brought us up single-handed, and never married again because she loved our father all her life. She was an admirable, saintly and completely unworldly woman. And now it was on this helpless woman that everything depended. She and father had attended Briusov's [literature] courses, but she did not get a diploma because I had already been born and my sister was on the way. Despite her education, my mother could never fulfil her potential, although I do know something about her literary work (I discovered some of her prose sketches). Without this disaster, things could have turned out very differently. But as she had no means of support, she became a proofreader for a printing press, where she worked until she reached retirement age. I find it simply unbelievable that she managed to afford an education for both myself and my sister. In spite of the situation, I was able to study painting and sculpture, which had to be paid for, so where did she get the money? I also studied music, and mother paid for a teacher before, during and after the war. I was supposed to become a musician, but that wasn't what I wanted. Of course an outsider might presume that anyone from an intellectual family would always have some kind of income at their disposal. But that was absolutely not the case: we used to walk around literally barefoot. In summer, because we simply didn't have any shoes, our feet were bare, and in winter I wore my mother's felt boots. Poverty doesn't describe our situation: it was nothing short of a beggar's life. If it hadn't been for my mother...I simply owe her everything. She had enormous influence on me. More than that: my whole world is bound up with my mother. That wasn't really clear to me during her lifetime; I became fully conscious of it only after her death. I made *Mirror* while she was still alive. Although it was conceived as a film about her, it seemed to me that I was actually making it about myself, just as Tolstoy had written *Childhood, Boyhood, Youth*. It was only later that I realized *Mirror* was not about me but about mother.

Source: Transcript of a talk given by Tarkovsky with Jerzy Illg and Leonard Noiger in Stockholm in 1985, during the filming of *The Sacrifice*. First published in Polish in the newspaper *Rzeczpospolita*, and in Russian in *Iskusstvo Kino* 1989, vol. 2, p. 113.

DIARY NOTE, 10 JULY 1981, MOSCOW

Another miracle. Despite everything, strange and wonderful miracles do sometimes happen to me.

I went to the cemetery today, to Mama's grave. A cramped little enclosure, a small bench, a simple grave with a wooden cross. The wild strawberries are putting out shoots. I prayed to God, wept, complained to Mama, and asked her to pray for me, to intercede...

Because really, life has become completely unbearable. If it weren't for Andriushka, death would seem the only tenable idea.

As I was leaving Mama I picked a wild strawberry leaf from her grave. It drooped on the way home, so I put it into warm water and the leaf revived. And I felt calmer and purer in my soul.

And suddenly there was a phone-call from Rome. It was Norman, to say that the Italians are coming here on the 20th. Of course it was Mama. I don't doubt it for a second. My dear, good Mama...my darling...thank you. And how guilty I feel towards you.

Source: *Time Within Time: The Diaries 1970–1986*, translated by Kitty Hunter-Blair, Calcutta, 1991, p. 284

A LETTER TO HIS FATHER

16/09/83

Dear Father

I'm very sad you have the impression that I've chosen the role of 'exile' and am almost on the point of abandoning my Russia...I don't know who stands to gain from this interpretation of the difficult situation I'm in, 'thanks' to years of persecution by the management of Goskino, particularly its chairman, Yermash. I believe he will have to answer for his actions to the Soviet government.

Maybe you haven't been counting, but I was out of work for about seventeen of the twenty plus years I worked in Soviet cinema.

Goskino did not want me to work!

During all that time I was persecuted, and the last straw was the scandal at Cannes caused by Bondarchuk's dishonourable behaviour. As a member of the jury and at the instigation of the authorities, he tried (in vain, it's true) to do everything to prevent me from winning a prize (I won three) for *Nostalgia*. I consider this film to be highly patriotic, and many of the ideas you hurl at me with such bitter reproach are expressed in it. Ask Yermash for permission to watch it, and you will understand and agree with me.

The leadership's desire to trample my feelings in the mud is part of their undoubted and passionate dream of getting rid of me, of washing their hands of me and my art, which is of no use to them whatsoever.

When hardly any of Mayakovsky's colleagues attended the exhibition to mark twenty years of his work, the poet took this as a cruel and unjust attack, and many literary scholars believe this was one of the main reasons why he shot himself.

When I celebrated my fiftieth birthday, not only was there no exhibition, but there was not even an announcement or congratulations in our journal of cinematography, which is always the case for every member of the Union of Soviet Film-Makers. But even this is unimportant; there are many reasons, all of them a humiliation. You simply do not know what has been going on.

Anyway, I have no intention of going away for long. I'm asking my bosses for passports for myself, Larisa, Andrusha and his grandmother, with whom I could live abroad for three years in order to fulfil – or rather live out – my cherished dream: staging the opera *Boris Godunov* at Covent Garden in London and *Hamlet* in the cinema. That's what my letter was about – a request to Goskino and the Department of Culture. I've still not had a reply.

I'm sure my government will grant me permission, both to undertake this work and for Andrusha and his grandmother, neither of whom I've seen for 18 months, to come here.

I'm sure the government won't start insisting on some other inhumane and unjust response. Its authority is so great that in my current situation it's absurd to believe I'm forcing it into the only possible answer. I have no other option: I cannot allow myself to be totally humiliated, and my letter is a request, not a demand. As for my feelings of patriotism, watch *Nostalgia* (if they'll show it to you), then you'll agree with me about my feelings for my country.

I'm sure everything will end well. I shall finish my work here and come back to Moscow very soon with Anna Semyonovna, Andrey and Larisa to embrace you and all our family, even if I (no doubt) remain in Moscow with no work. For me that's nothing new.

I'm sure my government won't refuse my modest request.

Should the unlikely happen, there'll be a terrible scandal. Heaven forbid, I don't want that, as you yourself know.

I'm not a dissident, I'm an artist who has made a contribution to the glorious treasure house of Soviet cinema. And I suspect I'm not the last.

(In *Soviet Film*, one talentless critic who had been coached by the authorities belatedly referred to me as great.) And I earned more money (in foreign currency) for my government than all the Bondarchuks put together.

Yet at the time my family were going hungry. That's why I can't accept this unfair and inhumane attitude towards me. I've remained a Soviet artist and shall continue to do so, no matter what the villains who are forcing me abroad are now saying.

With all my love, and wishing you health and strength. See you soon.

Your unhappy, worn-out son, Andrey Tarkovsky

P.S. Lara sends her love.

ON THE APOCALYPSE

A lecture given at St James's Church, Piccadilly, 18 July 1984

I am not accustomed to giving talks like the one I am about to give, in a place like a church. In fact, I am a little uncertain about my worldly concepts. However, I do not intend to deliver an expert report, but simply to reflect on what the Apocalypse means for me as an artist, which I think will save the situation and demonstrate why I have decided to stand up here today.

The very fact of my involvement in this festival is in my view quite apocalyptic, in the sense that if someone had told me it was possible a few months ago, I would not have believed them. However, my life has recently taken a somewhat apocalyptic turn, and so this step now seems logical and natural.

The Apocalypse is perhaps the greatest poetic work ever created. It is a phenomenon which essentially expresses all the laws imposed on mankind from on high. We know that through the ages people have argued over different readings of this or that excerpt from the Revelation of Saint John the Divine. In other words, broadly speaking, we are accustomed to the Revelation being interpreted and explained. In my view, this is precisely what should not be done, because the Apocalypse cannot be interpreted. There are no symbols in the Apocalypse: it is an image, and if a symbol can be interpreted, an image cannot. A symbol can be decoded, or rather a particular meaning can be ascribed to it, whereas an image is not something we can understand but something we can perceive and accept, for it has an infinite number of possible interpretations. It expresses an infinite number of connections to the world, as it were, to the absolute, to infinity. The Apocalypse is the last link in this chain, in this book; the final link completing the human Odyssey, in the spiritual sense of the word.

We live in very troubled times, which grow more difficult every year. Knowing something of history, though, we might recall that people have often talked of apocalyptic times being nigh. The Bible says: 'Blessed is he that reads, and they that hear the words of this prophecy, and keep those things which are written therein: for the time is at hand.' Nonetheless, the timing is so obviously vague that we cannot determine with any accuracy when what John writes about will occur. It could be tomorrow, it could be in a millennium. This is the meaning of the spiritual state of man; man should be aware of his responsibility for his own life. It is unimaginable that the Revelation originated when our time was already up. Thus no conclusions on timing can be drawn from the text of the Apocalypse.

You will no doubt have noticed that the Apocalypse contains many precise numbers and dates. The number of the sacrificed is given, and the number of the righteous. But in my opinion, this means absolutely nothing; it is a kind of image system to be perceived on an emotional level. Numbers and precise times are important to give us a sense of man's fate, a sense that we know the future. To give you an example, as a child I loved the book *Robinson Crusoe* and found the list of what was thrown ashore and what Robinson Crusoe rescued particularly appealing. We live in a material world and keep insisting that space and time are realities. In other words, we live within the boundaries of this phenomenon or rather these phenomena and are very sensitive to them, because they define our physical limits. But as we know, man was created in the image and likeness of God, and thus has freedom of will and the ability to create. In recent times, and for a fairly extended period, we have asked ourselves: is creativity in general not sinful? Why should this question arise, if we know for certain that creativity reminds us that we ourselves were created, that we have one Father? Why should an idea arise that I would term sacrilegious? Because the cultural crisis of the last hundred years has led to the artist being able to exist without any spiritual concepts whatsoever, with creativity as a kind of instinct. After all, we know that some animals have a sense of the aesthetic and can create something in the formal, natural sense, like a honeycomb, say, which bees create to put honey in. Artists have come to regard the talent they have been given as their property, hence their right to believe that their talent puts them under no obligation. This explains the lack of spiritual content in modern art. Art becomes either some kind of formalist search, or a commodity for sale. I need not tell you that cinema is top of the list here since, as you know, it was born at the end of the last century in a market aimed at pure profit.

I was recently in the Vatican Museum, which has a huge number of rooms dedicated to modern religious painting. It really needs to be seen, because it is appalling. I do not understand why these so-called works are displayed on the walls of such a museum, how they can satisfy religious people or especially the hierarchy of the Catholic church. It is quite amazing.

On the subject of the current crisis, the world we live in is all wrong. Man is born free and without fear, but our history consists in the desire to hide and protect ourselves from nature, which makes us crowd together unnecessarily. We mix with others not because we like company, or in order to derive pleasure from it, but so as to be less afraid. If our relationships are built on such a principle, then there is something wrong with our civilization. All the so-called technological progress that accompanies history has essentially created prostheses, making our arms longer, our vision sharper and enabling us to move more quickly. This last point is of fundamental importance: we can now move several times faster than in the last century, but we are no happier as a result. Our individuality, our personality has come into conflict with society. We have not developed in harmony; our spiritual development has lagged so far behind that we are now victims of an avalanche-like process of technological growth. We could not break free of the deluge even if we wanted to. When humankind needed and found new energy for technological development, we were not morally ready to use it for our own good. We are like savages who do not know what to do with an electron microscope: hammer nails with it, perhaps, or knock down walls? In any case, we are clearly slaves of this system, this machine that can no longer be stopped.

In terms of historical development, we have so come to distrust each other, to believe we cannot help each other (even if everything has been done in the name of common survival), that we ourselves, each one of us personally, are essentially failing to participate in the life of society. The individual is of no significance and so we are losing what we were given right at the outset: freedom of choice and free will. That is why I regard our civilization as wrong. The Russian philosopher and historian Nikolai Berdiaev puts it very well: there are two stages in the history of civilization. The first is the history of culture, when man's development is more or less harmonious and based on spiritual foundations; the second is when a chain reaction starts that is not subordinate to man's will, when forward motion spins out of control and society loses its culture.

What is the Apocalypse? As I said before, in my view it is an image of the human soul, with all its responsibilities and obligations. Each person undergoes what the Book of Revelation describes: that is, he or she cannot avoid it. Thus in the final analysis this is the reason why we can say that death and suffering are the same whether an individual suffers and dies or the cycle of history comes to an end and millions suffer and die, because man is only able to endure the pain that he finds manageable.

On the subject of our conformism, the Book of Revelation says: 'I know your works, that you are neither cold nor hot: I would that you were cold or hot. So then because you are lukewarm, and neither cold nor hot, I will spew you out of my mouth.' In other words, indifference and apathy are the same as sin, a crime against the Creator. On the other hand: 'Those whom I love, I reprove and discipline, so be zealous and repent.' In short, our repentance is by and large the beginning of the road. This meaning is grasped by different people in different ways and at different times. Take Dostoyevsky, for instance. One view is that he was a religious, Russian Orthodox writer who wrote about his own searchings and the characteristics of his own faith. My feeling is that this is not entirely true. Dostoyevsky made his great discoveries only because he was the first to become aware of and find expression for the problem of spiritual impoverishment. His heroes suffer from their inability to believe. They want to, but they have lost the wherewithal for belief, their consciences have atrophied. And as each year passes Dostoyevsky becomes increasingly accessible, fashionable even, precisely because the problem is growing more and more widespread, because belief is the hardest thing of all. As a general principle, we cannot hope for God's grace. Of course, happy is the man who has experienced that state, but by no means everyone can attain it. The most important thing for us to feel free and happy is lack of fear.

In some wondrous way, all these problems are covered in the Apocalypse. In the end, the Apocalypse is the story of destiny, the destiny of man who, as an individual, cannot live apart from society. When nature saves a species from extinction, the animals are not aware of the drama of existence. And in so far as we humans choose our own path, thanks to free will, we cannot save everyone but can only save ourselves. This is how we are able to save others. We do not know what love is, we treat ourselves with appalling disregard. We misunderstand what it is to love oneself, we are even uncomfortable with the concept because we think that to love oneself means being egotistical. This is wrong, because love is sacrifice, and even if man is not aware of it, it is noticeable to an observer, a third person. Of course, you know that, for the Bible says: 'Love thy neighbour as thyself.' In other words, love for oneself is a foundation for emotion, a yardstick, not just because man has understood himself and the meaning of his life, but because one should always start with oneself.

I do not mean to say that I have succeeded in all the things I am discussing now; indeed, I am far from holding myself up as an example. On the contrary, I believe that all my misfortunes stem from not following my own advice! The trouble is that the facts are clear, and where our skewed view of things will lead us is also clear. However, it would be wrong to think that the Apocalypse's only message is of punishment. Perhaps its main message is one of hope. Even though the time is near, and for each of us individually it really is very near, for all of us together it is never too late. The Apocalypse is terrifying for each person individually, but for all of us together it brings hope. This is where the meaning of the Revelation lies. In the final analysis, this dialectic, expressed metaphorically, is such a source of inspiration for the artist that you cannot help but marvel at the number of points of support to be found in it, no matter what one's emotional state.

On the destruction of time and space, their transition to a new state, the Bible expresses it beautifully. On the disappearance of space, it says: 'The stars in the sky fell to the earth like a fig tree drops its fruit when it is shaken by a strong wind. And the sky vanished like a scroll being rolled up.' A sky that vanished, like a rolled-up scroll! I have never read anything finer. And then this, about what happened after the removal of the seventh seal. What can any artist say about the means used to express it! How can not only that tension, but that crossing point be expressed? 'And when he (i.e. the Lamb) had opened the seventh seal, there was silence in heaven for about half an hour.' As a friend of mine said, words would be superfluous here. The seventh seal is removed, and what happens? Nothing. Silence ensues. It is incredible! In this instance the lack of image is the strongest image you could imagine. It is like a miracle!

There is a book in which Carlos Castanada writes the story of how he studied with a Mexican shaman. It is an incredibly interesting book, but that is not really the issue. A rumour started that there was no shaman and this was not memoir, but that Castaneda had invented the whole thing: his method of self-instruction, which he wants to use to change the world, the shaman and his methods. Yet this does nothing to detract from the core point; on the contrary, it reinforces it. In other words, if all this is the invention of one man, it is even more of a miracle than if it had really happened. In brief, my thinking is that in the final analysis, the artistic image is always a miracle.

Here is another quote from the Book of Revelation, and what it has to say about time is also beautifully put: 'And the angel whom I saw stand upon the sea and upon the earth lifted up his hand to heaven and swore by him who lives for ever and ever, who created the heavens and all that is in them, the earth and all that is in it, and the sea and all that is in it, and said that there should be time no longer.' It sounds like a promise, like hope. Nevertheless, a mystery remains, because there is one place in the Apocalypse that looks very odd in the context of a Book of Revelation: 'And when the seven thunders had uttered their voices, I was about to write: and I heard a voice from heaven saying unto me, Seal up those things which the seven thunders uttered, and write them not.' I wonder what John concealed from us, why he said he had sealed something up? Why this strange remark, this sudden reversal between the angel and John the Divine? What was it that man should not know? After all, the whole point of the Revelation was for man to know. Perhaps the very concept of knowledge makes us unhappy? You remember: 'For in much wisdom is much grief'? Why? Or was it necessary to conceal our fate from us, a particular moment of destiny? I for one would not be able to live if I knew the prophecy of my life. In other words, life would lose all meaning if I knew how it was going to end, my own personal fate. This detail has an amazing, superhuman nobility, which leaves man feeling as defenceless as a baby, yet at the same time protected. It is done so that our knowledge remains incomplete, so as not to cast a blight on eternity, so hope remains. In man's ignorance there is hope. Not knowing is noble, knowing is vulgar. Therefore the solicitude expressed in the Apocalypse gives me hope more than it frightens me.

I now ask myself the question: what should I do, having read the Book of Revelation? Obviously I can no longer be the same as before, not just because I have changed, but because I have been told, and knowing what I now know I am obliged to change.

On this point, I am beginning to think that the art I am engaged in is only possible if it is not about my personal expression, but brings together what I have assimilated from my interactions with other people. Art becomes sinful as soon as I start using it in my own interests. The main thing is that I have ceased to interest myself. Perhaps this is where my love for myself starts.

I would like to thank those who invited me here today, although I had no wish to tell you anything new. By reflecting like this in your presence, I wanted to feel the significance of this moment and this process, and I got what I wanted. You have given me the opportunity to reach some conclusions and turn over some ideas, because it is not possible to think about these things on one's own. Also, I should say that, in preparing to make my new film, getting ready to take a first step in that direction, it is very clear to me that I ought to approach it not as piece of free creation, but as a deliberate step, a forced act, where the work can no longer bring satisfaction but is an arduous, even oppressive duty. To tell the truth, I have never thought that an artist could be happy during the process of creation. Or is that the wrong word? Happy? No, never. Man does not live to be happy. There are far more important things than happiness.

Thank you very much.
(*Prolonged applause.*)

Source: Translated from a transcription published by V. Ishimova and R. Sheiko in *Iskusstvo Kino* 1989, vol. 2, pp. 96–100, accompanied by the following note: 'In 1984 we were in London, and came across tape recordings of "On the Apocalypse" and two other meetings Tarkovsky had with London audiences. When he learned of this, he passed on a request via friends: that when we returned to Moscow, we made copies of these recordings and give them to his son. We carried out Tarkovsky's wishes.'

QUESTIONNAIRE
(DIARY EXTRACT, 3 JANUARY 1974)

1. Your favourite landscape?
   Dawn, summer, mist
2. Season?
   Autumn, dry, sunny
3. Musical work?
   Bach, *St. John's Passion*
4. Russian prose work (novel, novella)
   Crime and Punishment, *Death of Ivan Ilych*
5. Foreign prose work (novel)
   Doctor Faustus
6. Novella (Russian)
   Bunin, *Sunstroke*
7. Novella (foreign)
   Maupassant, *Tonio Kruger* by Thomas Mann
8. Favourite colour
   Green
9. Poet
   Pushkin
10. Film director (Russian)
    none
11. Film director (foreign)
    Bresson
12. Do you like children?
    Very much
13. What is a woman's driving-force?
    Submission, humiliation in the name of love
14. And a man's?
    Creation
15. The colour of a woman's hair?
    Red
16. Favourite clothes
17. Favourite period

Source: *Time Within Time: The Diaries 1970–1986*, translated by Kitty Hunter-Blair, Calcutta, 1991, p. 89

Family Album

Tarkovsky's mother, Maria Vishnyakova Tarkovskaya, Zavrazhye, 1932

FAMILY ALBUM AND POLAROIDS: INTRODUCTORY NOTE

The photographs of the Tarkovsky family are taken from the album Andrey compiled before making the autobiographical film *Mirror*. Dating from between 1928 and 1948, they cover the lives of his father Arseny Aleksandrovich Tarkovsky and his mother Maria Vishnyakova Tarkovskaya, little Andrey himself and his sister Marina. They are in no particular order and offer insights into their family life in Yurevets and Zavarazhye, Tarkovsky's birthplace in the district of Ivanovo, as well as during their summer holidays in the country or in Moscow.

The Polaroids of Russia were taken by Andrey Tarkovsky in 1981, the year in which he last visited his homeland.

The epilogue consists of a sequence of Polaroids that Andrey Tarkovsky took in Italy during the filming of *Nostalgia* in 1981–82.

In Tarkovsky's birthplace of Zavrazhye, 1930

Tarkovsky's mother, 1932

Young Andrey and his mother, Yurevets, 1933

Mother and son, Yurevets, 1933

Tarkovsky's father, Arseny Aleksandrovich Tarkovsky, Kineshma, 1928

Moscow, 1929–30

1930s

1930s

As a soldier on the front, *c.* 1943

Father and son in Maloyaroslavets, summer 1934

Mother and son, Yurevets, 1935

With his father, mother and sister Marina, 1935

Andrey and his mother, Yurevets, 1935

Yurevets, 1933

Cottage in Yurevets, 1935

Annuskha (Anna Yakovlevna Andriyakova), Tarkovsky's nanny during the summer holidays, Krasnyi, 1935

Father and son in Maloyaroslavets, summer 1934

Andrey and his uncle Lyova (Lev Vladimirovich Gornung), Maloyaroslavets, summer 1934

Andrey and his sister Marina, Yurevets, 1937

Andrey's cousin Vera Sergeyevna Shopotko, Moscow, 1937

Andrey and his sister Marina, Moscow, 1939

Andrey, Moscow, 1937–38

Marina dressed in a Japanese costume, Moscow, January 1941

Andrey dressed as a pirate, Moscow, January 1941

Andrey and his mother, Moscow, 1947

Andrey and his cousin Vera, Moscow, 1947

Andrey and his father, Moscow, 1947

Andrey on his 16th birthday, 4 April 1948, with Grishka the cat

Andrey with Kapa the cat, Moscow, 1947

Tarkovsky's father Arseny, Moscow, 1937

Russian Polaroids

In the country: the village of Myasnoye, 28 August 1981

ABOVE: The actor Anatoli Solonitsyn, Moscow, 22 May 1981
BELOW: Myasnoye, 2 October 1981

ABOVE: Andrey A. Tarkovsky, 28 August 1981
BELOW: Larisa Tarkovskaya, Moscow, 3 August 1980

Andrey A. Tarkovsky and Dak, September 1980

Andrey A. Tarkovsky and Dak, Moscow, 10 May 1980

ABOVE: Myasnoye, 8 September 1980
BELOW: Larisa Tarkovskaya and Dak, 29 September 1981

Myasnoye, 26 September 1981

Dak, Myasnoye, 26 September 1981

Dak, Myasnoye, 26 September 1981

Myasnoye, 26 September 1981

Larisa Tarkovskaya and Dak, Myasnoye, 26 September 1981

Italian Polaroids

On the set of *Nostalgia*, Otricoli, October 1982

On the set of *Nostalgia*, Bagno Vignoni, 6 November 1972

Bagno Vignoni, San Quirico d'Orcia, Tuscany, 8–20 August 1979

Bagno Vignoni, 8–20 August 1979

Hotel Le Terme, Bagno Vignoni, 8–20 August 1979

Hotel Le Terme, Bagno Vignoni, 8–20 August 1979

San Gregorio, 24 November 1983

Larisa Tarkovskaya, San Gregorio, 1983

ABOVE: Monterano, 28 April 1982
BELOW: Cinematographer Giuseppe Lanci, Monterano, 28 April 1982

Hotel San Domenico, Taormina, Sicily, 19–26 July 1980

Taormina, Sicily, 19–26 July 1980

Taormina, Sicily, 19–26 July 1980

Biography

COMPILED BY HANS-JOACHIM SCHLEGEL

1932
Andrey Arsenyevich Tarkovsky is born in Zavrazhye, a village some 300 kilometres northeast of Moscow, near Yurevets, in the Ivanovo region. He is the eldest son of Maria Ivanovna Vishnyakova, a proofreader, and Arseny Aleksandrovich Tarkovsky, a well-known poet and translator. Both parents come from aristocratic families, and his grandfather, Aleksandr Karlovich Tarkovsky, had been an active revolutionary who belonged to the radical group Narodnaia Volia (People's Will). In autumn the family moves to Moscow.

1935
Tarkovsky's father leaves his family and from 1937 lives nearby with his new wife. He returns from the war having lost a leg. With his sister Marina, Andrey is brought up by his mother, who never remarries. The trauma of this separation and of a childhood overshadowed by the war is re-imagined in *Mirror*, in which his mother makes an appearance and his father recites some of his own poems.

1940
The family spends the summer in a dacha in the village of Ignatievo, where Tarkovsky will later film *Mirror*.

1941
In May, Andrey, his mother, sister and grandmother are in the village of Bitiukovo, on the Rozhyshche river. When war breaks out they return to Moscow. On 29 August 1941 they are evacuated to Yurevets.

1943
The family returns to Moscow.

1947–48
At the end of November Andrey falls ill with tuberculosis and is taken to a children's hospital in Moscow, where he makes a big impression as a keen pianist and actor.

1951
In August he enters the Moscow Institute of Oriental Studies to learn Arabic but gives up the course in winter 1953 without graduating. He is regarded as an eccentrically dressed, jazz-crazy *stilyaga*, a hipster member of Moscow's rebel subculture. At the instigation of his mother, who is very concerned about the direction he is taking, he joins a geological expedition to search for gold and diamonds along the Kureika river in the far eastern Turukhansk Taiga, the part of Siberia to which Stalin had once been banished.

1954
In April he returns to Moscow, and on 23 June applies to study at VGIK (Moscow Cinema Institute).

In August he begins his course in film direction, attending master classes given by Mikhail Romm, who had inspired the innovative 'Thaw' generation. His favourite directors include Aleksandr Dovzhenko, Ingmar Bergman, Robert Bresson and Luis Buñuel. He writes a critical analysis of Sergei Yutkevich's *The Great Warrior Skanderbeg* (1954), which had been awarded a prize at Cannes, and plans the short film *Concentrate* (1958), which captures impressions from his geological expeditions. With fellow student Aleksandr Gordon, who later marries his sister Marina, he makes two short films: *The Killers* (1956, an adaptation of a Hemingway short story, in which he, Gordon and Vasili Shukshin play various roles), and *There Will Be No Leave Today* (1958).

With Andrei Konchalovsky he writes screenplays for *Antarctica – Distant Country* (1959 – though the film is never made), his diploma film *The Steamroller and the Violin* (1961) and *Andrei Rublev* (1964–66). Although he is not credited, he is also co-writer with Boris Dobrodeev and Chingiz Aitmatov of the screenplay for Konchalovsky's debut film *The First Teacher* (1964). His friendship with Konchalovsky later ends amid increasingly bitter disagreements.

1957
He marries Irma Raush, a Russian-German fellow student, who plays the part of the mother in *Ivan's Childhood* and the idiot girl in *Andrei Rublev*.

1961
His gains a distinction from VGIK and is employed by Mosfilm as a 'Director of the Third Category'. *The Steamroller and the Violin* takes first prize at the New York Student Film Festival. He appears in Marlen Khutsiev's film about Soviet youth, *I Am Twenty* and writes a treatment for *Andrei's Passion* (later known as *Andrei Rublev*). In the summer he begins shooting his debut feature, *Ivan's Childhood.*

1962
On 6 April *Ivan's Childhood* premieres at the Centralny Cinema in Moscow; in August it is awarded the Golden Lion at the Venice Film Festival. It takes first prize in San Francisco and Acapulco and he travels with it to India and Ceylon. Only a few copies are distributed in the USSR and the heated debates prefigure the conflicts and impediments that will greet his work. Jean-Paul Sartre defends the film against left-wing criticism that it is petit-bourgeois in *L'Unità*, the mouthpiece of the Italian Communist Party.

On 30 September 1962, Andrey's first son Arseny is born.

He signs the contract for *Andrei Rublev* and begins work on the screenplay.

1963
In February he is accepted into the Union of Soviet Film-Makers. On 18 December he hands in the 'literary screenplay' for his *Rublev* project.

1964
On 24 April the 'director's script' for *Andrey's Passion* (later *Andrei Rublev*) is finished and a version is published in *Iskusstvo Kino* (1964, nos 4–5). On 9 September he begins preparatory work for shooting, which begins in November, though filming is frequently interrupted by bureaucracy.

He takes part in debates held in the Sovremennik Theatre in Moscow, where there is the possibility of him doing some work. Instead, he directs the radio play *Turnabout* – an adaptation of a short story by William Faulkner, which had been filmed by Howard Hawks in 1933. The main character, played by Nikita Mikhalkov, is a young English naval officer in the First World War.

In August he is a member of the jury at the Venice Film Festival.

1965
Turnabout is ready for transmission in spring but is condemned as 'pacifist' and given only a single broadcast in the Transural region. Years later, a wider audience is reached via a posthumous broadcast on Radio Moscow on 26 December 1987.

During the filming of *Andrei Rublev,* Andrey meets Larisa Pavlovna Kizilova, who will become his second wife.

1966
Filming of *Andrei Rublev* is completed on 26 August. In December the film is screened privately at Mosfilm and the Union of Soviet Film-Makers. As a result of numerous objections (e.g. to the 'naturalistically cruel' closing scenes), the film is cut from 5,624 m to 5,250 m, and when it is eventually distributed in 1971 it has been further reduced to 5,076 m.

1967
Under the titles *Confession* and *A White, White Day* (a line from one of his father's poems), he writes the first drafts of what is to become *Mirror* (with Aleksandr Misharin as co-writer).

In Chisinau in Moldova he works on Aleksandr Gordon's film *Sergei Lazo* as co-writer and acting the role of an officer of the White Guard.

1968
He finishes the screenplay for *Mirror* and submits treatments for this and for a film of the science-fiction novel *Solaris* by Stanislaw Lem. From October, he works on the *Solaris* script with Friedrich Gorenstein.

1969
At the Cannes Film Festival, a copy of *Andrei Rublev* that has already been purchased by a French distributor is shown out of competition, despite Soviet protests. The film wins the FIPRESCI international film critics' prize, but is still banned in the Soviet Union.

He continues to work on the screenplay for *Solaris* as well as co-writing Leonid Kocharian's film *One Chance in a Thousand* and working uncredited with Andrei Konchalovsky on the screenplay for the Uzbek film *Tashkent, City of Bread* by Shukhrat Abbasov.

1970
He begins filming *Solaris* with little interference from the authorities, who are expecting a science-fiction film with the potential to reach an international market.

On 18 June he divorces his first wife Irma Raush and marries Larisa Pavlovna Kizilova, who gives birth to his second son Andrey on 7 August. He and Andrei Konchalovsky co-write the Kazakh film *The End of Ataman* by Shaken Aimanov.

1971
On 19 October *Andrei Rublev* is finally licensed for distribution in the Soviet Union. He works with Friedrich Gorenstein on the screenplay for *House with a Little Tower*, but the film is never made.

1972
On 20 March *Solaris* is licensed for distribution and in May it wins the Grand Prix du Jury at Cannes; it is later named Best Film of the Year at the London Festival of Festivals.

In July Mosfilm classify him as 'Director of the First Category'.

He gives advanced courses in film direction in Moscow and in autumn travels to Italy, Brussels, Luxembourg, Bruges and Paris.

1973
The Soviet premiere of *Solaris* takes place at the Mir Cinema in Moscow. He travels to screenings in Uruguay and Argentina and from the end of February until 10 March is in East Germany, where he considers the possibility of filming Thomas Mann's *The Magic Mountain* and visits the Pergamon Museum in Berlin and Dresden Art Gallery. In Potsdam he suffers a heart attack. After the positive response to screenings of *Andrei Rublev* in East Germany, the Soviet ban on exporting the film is lifted.

He and Friedrich Gorenstein write an adaptation of *Ariel*, a novella by Soviet science-fiction writer Aleksandr Belyaev, but the film is never made. In September he begins filming *Mirror*. He is invited by Mark Zakharov to direct a production of *Hamlet* at the Lenkom Theatre in Moscow.

1974
He finishes filming *Mirror* in March and then begins the long and painstaking task of editing it.

In April he goes to Rome for the Italian premiere of *Solaris*.

In July the authorities reject *Mirror*. The film is given a private screening at the Union of Soviet Film-Makers in autumn, and extracts from the subsequent discussions are published in *Iskusstvo Kino* (1975, no. 4).

He writes preliminary sketches for a film version of Dostoyevsky's *The Idiot* and works as artistic adviser on Bagrat Oganesyan's Armenian film *Sour Grapes*. Together with Mukhtar Auezov, he writes the screenplays for Tolomush Okeyev's Kirghiz film *The Ferocious One* and for the Uzbek director Ali Khamraev's *Sardor* (not made).

1975
Mirror is shown in three out-of-town Moscow cinemas, but is not allowed to be entered for the Cannes Film Festival.

He writes more outlines for *The Idiot* and begins rehearsals for *Hamlet*, with Anatoli Solonitsyn in the title role. He also writes the script for *Hoffmanniana*, based on the life and work of E.T.A. Hoffmann.

1976
He works with Arkady and Boris Strugatsky on the screenplay for *Stalker* (based on their science-fiction novella *Roadside Picnic*).

Hoffmanniana is published in *Iskusstvo Kino* (no. 8).

In December the dress rehearsal for *Hamlet* is held in the Lenkom Theatre.

1977
Premiere of *Hamlet* and the start of filming *Stalker* in the area surrounding Chernobyl, Japan and Estonia, where he also looks for locations for *Hoffmanniana* and acts as adviser for *Karikakramäng*, an anthology film by young Estonian directors Peeter Urbla, Toomas Tahvel and Peeter Simm.

The first filmed version of *Stalker* is technically flawed and unusable so the film has to be reshot.

1978
He travels to France, where *Mirror* wins the award for Best Film of the Year. In April he suffers a heart attack.

1979
He finishes work on *Stalker*. In April he travels to Italy with a delegation of Soviet film-makers, followed by a second trip in summer for two months, as well as a visit to Poland. Together with the Uzbek director Zakir Sabitov, he writes the screenplay for the latter's film *Beware, Snakes!*

On 8 October his mother dies of cancer in Moscow.

1980
In January he is given the title 'People's Artist of the RSFSR'. He spends spring and summer in Italy, where he works with Tonino Guerra on the documentary *Tempo di viaggio* and on the screenplay for *Nostalgia*. Luchino Visconti presents him with the David di Donatello award for *Mirror*.

In autumn he returns to Moscow.

1981
He attends screenings of *Stalker* in England and Scotland and in April travels to Sweden. Despite an offer of asylum there, he returns to Moscow.

1982
In January he travels to Georgia and Leningrad, where he meets Aleksandr Sokurov.

On 6 March he leaves for Italy. He finishes *Tempo di viaggio* and starts filming *Nostalgia* as an Italian-Soviet co-production.

At the end of the year, his wife Larisa joins him in Italy.

1983
At Cannes in May *Nostalgia* fails to win the Palme d'Or as expected but is awarded the Prize for Best Direction (jointly with Robert Bresson's *L'argent*), Special Jury Prize and FIPRESCI Prize. Tarkovsky suspects that there has been a conspiracy, with the Soviet adjudicator Sergei Bondarchuk acting under instructions from the authorities. In May he is fired by Mosfilm on the grounds of 'unauthorized absence from the workplace'.

In September he attends a film festival in Telluride, Colorado.

In November his production of Mussorgsky's opera *Boris Godunov* premieres in London.

He begins work on the screenplay for *The Sacrifice*.

1984
On 10 July he announces at a press conference in Milan that he will not be returning to the USSR.

In autumn he travels to Stockholm, the Netherlands and West Berlin, where he is awarded a grant by the DAAD and welcomed as a guest by the Künstlerhaus Bethanien.

1985
In February Ullstein Verlag publishes *Die versiegelte Zeit. Gedanken zur Kunst, zur Ästhetik und Poetik des Films*, a German translation of interviews that mostly appeared from 1967 to 1984 in *Iskusstvo Kino*. The book is published in the UK as *Sculpting in Time* in 1987. In spring he starts filming *The Sacrifice* in Sweden. In September he travels to Florence, returning to Stockholm in November.

On 13 December he is told he has lung cancer.

1986
On 8 January he begins treatment at a French cancer clinic. On 19 January the Soviet authorities give his son Andrey and Andrey's grandmother a travel permit.

On 9 May *The Sacrifice* premieres at the Astoria Cinema in Stockholm. On 19 May his son Andrey Andreyevich accepts on his behalf the Grand Prix du Jury at the Cannes Film Festival, where the USSR entry was Bondarchuk's *Boris Godunov*, and the hoped-for Palme d'Or went to Roland Joffé's *The Mission*.

From 7 July to 17 August he stays at the Öschelbronn Clinic near Baden-Baden. From 18 August he is in Italy with his family – first in Ansedonia and then in Cala Piccola. On the night of 28 October he returns by train to the cancer clinic in Paris, where he dies on 29 December.

1987
On 5 January he is given a funeral blessing in the Church of Alexander Nevsky, Paris, and is buried in the Russian Cemetery at Sainte Geneviève des Bois, near Paris.

1990
Andrey Tarkovsky is posthumously awarded the Order of Lenin.

Other Works

THEATRE, OPERA AND RADIO

1964
Turnabout (*Polnyi povorot krugom*)
Gosteleradio, Moscow
Radio adaptation of William Faulkner's short story 'Turnabout'
Script and director: Andrey Tarkovsky
Music: Vyacheslav Ovchinnikov
Script assistant: Aleksandr Misharin
Editor: Konstantin Kuzakov
Cast: Nikita Mikhalkov (Midshipman Claude Hope), Aleksandr Lazarev (Captain Bogard)
Following a single transmission for listeners in the Transural region, the next broadcast was not until 26 December 1987 (three days after the first anniversary of Tarkovsky's death) on Radio Moscow.

1977
Hamlet by William Shakespeare
(Russian translation by Boris Pasternak)
Lenkom Theatre, Moscow
Director: Andrey Tarkovsky
Music: Eduard Artemiev
Cast: Anatoli Solonitsyn (Hamlet), Margarita Terekhova (Gertrude), Vladimir *Shiryaev* (Claudius), Inna Churikova (Ophelia), Vsevolod Larionov (Polonius), Nikolai Karachentsov (Laertes)

1983
Boris Godunov, opera by Modest Mussorgsky
Royal Opera House, Covent Garden, London
Director: Andrey Tarkovsky
Conductors: Claudio Abbado, James Lockhart
Art direction: Nikolai Dvigubsky
Lighting: Robert Bryan
Cast: Robert Lloyd (Boris Godunov), Jonathan Summers (Andrei Shchelkalov), Philip Langridge (Prince Shinsky), Fiona Kimm (Feodor)

AS CO-DIRECTOR

1956
The Killers (*Ubiytsy*)
Student film, 20 minutes
Directors: Andrey Tarkovsky, Aleksandr Gordon, Marika Beiku
Script: Andrey Tarkovsky, Aleksandr Gordon
Costumes: Aleksandr Rybin, Alfredo Álvarez
Cast: Yuli Fait, Aleksandr Gordon, Valentin Vinogradov, Yuri Dubrovin, Andrey Tarkovsky, Vasili Shukshin, Boris Novikov

1958
There Will Be No Leave Today (*Segodnia uvolnenia ne budet*)
Student film, 47 minutes
Directors: Andrey Tarkovsky, Aleksandr Gordon
Script: Andrey Tarkovsky, Aleksandr Gordon, I. Makhov
Production manager: Y. Kotoshev
Music: Yuri Matskevich
Cast: Aleksei Smirnov, Stanislav Liubshin, Andrey Tarkovsky

1983
Tempo di viaggio (*Voyage in Time*)
Documentary film, Italy, 62 minutes, colour
Script and directors: Tonino Guerra, Andrey Tarkovsky

AS ACTOR

1956
The Killers (see above). Tarkovsky plays a customer in a bar

1958
There Will Be No Leave Today (see above)

1965
I Am Twenty/The Ilyich Gate (*Mne dvadtsat let/Zastava Ilyicha*)
Guest at a student party
Director: Marlen Khutsiev

1967
Sergei Lazo
White Guard officer
Director: Aleksandr Gordon

AS WRITER AND CO-WRITER

1958
Concentrate (*Konsentrat*)

1959
Antarctica – Distant Country (*Antarktida, dalekaia strana*)
– not made
Script: Andrey Tarkovsky, Andrei Konchalovsky, Oleg Osetinsky

1964
The First Teacher (*Pervyi uchitel*)
Script: Andrey Tarkovsky (uncredited), Andrei Konchalovsky, Boris Dobrodeev, Chingiz Aimatov (based on his own story)
Director: Andrei Konchalovsky (Kyrgyzstan)

1967
Sergei Lazo
Script: Andrey Tarkovsky, Aleksandr Gordon
Director: Aleksandr Gordon (Moldova)

1969
One Chance in a Thousand (*Odin shans iz tysiachi*)
Script: Andrey Tarkovsky, Leonid Kocharian, Artur Makarov
Director: Bagrat Oganesyan, Leonid Kocharian (Armenia)
Also artistic advisor

1969
Tashkent, City of Bread (*Tashkent – gorod khlebnyi*)
Script based on the novel of the same name by Aleksandr Neverov: Andrey Tarkovsky (uncredited), Andrei Konchalovsky
Director: Shukhrat Abbasov (Uzbekistan)

1970
The End of Ataman (*Konec atamana*)
Script: Andrey Tarkovsky, Andrei Konchalovsky
Director: Shaken Aimanov (Kazakhstan)

1971
House with a Little Tower (*Domik s baschenkoj*) – not made
Script: Andrey Tarkovsky, Friedrich Gorenstein

1973
Ariel – not made
Script: Andrey Tarkovsky, Friedrich Gorenstein

1974
The Ferocious One (*Lyutyy*)
Script: Andrey Tarkovsky, Mukhtar Auezov (original short story)
Director: Tolomush Okeyev (Kyrgyzstan)

Sardor, written for the Uzbek director Ali Khamraev – not made

1979
Beware, Snakes! (*Beregis, zmey!*)
Script: Andrey Tarkovsky
Director: Zakir Sabitov (Uzbekistan)

1981
The Dream
Script: Andrey Tarkovsky, written for Armenfilm – not made

AS ARTISTIC ADVISOR

1969
One Chance in a Thousand (see above)

1973
Sour Grapes (*Terpkiy vinograd*)
Director: Bagrat Oganesyan (Armenia)

1978
Karikakramäng (*Gadanie na romashke*)
Estonian anthology film, with sections directed by Peeter Urbla, Toomas Tahvel and Peeter Simm

Bibliography

BOOKS BY ANDREY TARKOVSKY

Sculpting in Time: Reflections on the Cinema, trans. Kitty Hunter-Blair, London: The Bodley Head, 1986; revised ed.: London: Faber & Faber, 1989

'Hoffmanniana', screenplay, trans. Natasha Synessios, in *Grand Street* 68, 1999 and *Andrei Tarkovsky Collected Screenplays*, trans. William Powell and Natasha Synessios, London: Faber & Faber, 1999

Opfer. Filmbuch, German trans. Rosemarie Tietze, Munich: Schirmer/Mosel, 1987

Time Within Time: The Diaries, 1970–1986, trans. Kitty Hunter-Blair, Calcutta: Seagull, 1991; London: Faber & Faber, 1994

Andrej Rubljow: Die Novelle, German trans. Ute Spengler, Berlin: Limes, 1992

Der Spiegel. Die Novelle und das Arbeitstagebuch zum Film, German trans. Kurt Baudisch and Ute Spengler, Berlin: Limes, 1993

Instant Light: Tarkovsky Polaroids, eds Giovanni Chiaramonte and Andrey A. Tarkovsky. London and New York: Thames & Hudson, 2006

SELECTED BOOKS ABOUT ANDREY TARKOVSKY

Larissa Tarkovskaya (with Luba Jurgenson), *Andrei Tarkovski*, Paris: Calmann-Lévy, 1989

Marina Tarkovskaya (ed.), *About Andrei Tarkovsky: Memoirs and Biographies*, Moscow: Progress Publishers, 1990

Marina Tarkovskaya, *Oskolki Zerkala* (*Pieces of Mirror*), 2nd edition, Moscow: Vagrius, 2006

Maya Turovskaya, *Tarkovsky: Cinema as Poetry*, trans. Natasha Ward; ed. Ian Christie, London and Boston: Faber & Faber, 1989

Peter W. Jansen, Wolfram Schütte (eds), *Andrej Tarkowskij*, Munich: Carl Hanser Verlag, 1987

Index

Page numbers in *italic* refer to illustrations.